MW01710324

My Child
My Responsibility

PUBLISHING LLC

Copyright © 2012 by Jonetta Smith
All rights reserved. No portion of this book may be reproduced-mechanically, electronically, or by any other means–including photocopying–without written permission of the publisher, except by a reviewer who may quote brief passages in a review.

Library of Congress Cataloging-in-Publication Data
Smith., Jonetta

TXU1-736-812

My Child, My Responsibility / by Jonetta Smith
ISBN 9780984036301

I. Parenting II. Family

Front cover, author, and family
photograph by *Pete Stenberg*
Book editing by *John Lennox*
Co-editor: *Jakina Smith*
Cover design & book layout by
Mary Valle-Cooper, Yorké Design Studio

Printed in the United States of America
First edition: February 2012

Acknowledgements

First, I want to give honor to God, the head of my life and my household. Thank you God, for giving me a desire to help others when I see them in need of help. Thank you for protecting me with your loving arms wrapped around me. You are awesome, God.

To my loving son Javonte: God gave you to me, and I thank him for the blessing. You have overcome stumbling blocks in your life that many children will never face. But through prayer, trials, and determination, you are a winner. Through your perseverance you continue to prove that God doesn't make mistakes. Thank you for assisting me with this project.

To my loving son Graylin II: God gave you to me, and I thank him for the blessing. You are a leader, and a strong young man. I believe you were here before this lifetime. Your calmness soothes my soul. The race is not given to the swift, but to the strong who endure until the end. Stay peaceful son, don't let nothing destroy your peace.

To my loving daughter, Ms. Jaylin: God gave you to me, and I thank him for the blessing. Oh, what joy I have with you. Don't you give in to circumstances. I'm proud to see you take on the challenge of losing weight. It was your own willingness to become more conscious of life that made you request my assistance in that journey. You go beyond higher heights. Continue to be strong and God will place you on solid ground. Whose baby—mommy's baby.

To my loving mother, Ms. Freddie Smith: you fought a good fight—keep your head pointed in God's direction. I thank you for the life you gave to me. Don't you worry anymore: I'm here to be your helping hand. Through all the rough surfaces, throughout your life's journey, God gave you favor and the devil is mad. Love you no doubt. I am a product you produced.

To my loving grandparents, Daniel and Irene Reeves (deceased): thank you for being the foundation of the family. We sometimes get off track, but your teaching and loving care helps us hold it together. Granny, I love you. I know you are smiling down on me, your pride and joy. You are my light, my rock, because of you, and my mother I'm here today. I hear your voice of wisdom at all times.

To my sister Cieara: love comes from within and then it spreads abroad. You are a single young lady without any children—that's rare to-day. Don't let anything sidetrack your dreams. Keep it moving little sis: the race is not given to the swift, but to the strong who endure until the end.

To my brother Nathan: I love you with all my heart. My niece needs her dad—please make a turn for the better, for you and for the sake of her future. All things are possible if you believe. Love you, my only niece, Ms. Shari Lashun.

To my brother/cousin Mr. Jerry: I love you with all my heart. Take time to cherish the precious moments with your children.

To my cousins Michael and Carol Geans, thank you for being a help to my mom with Nathan and I. Thank you for the fun times at the beach, the bike rides, and walks we took. Love you with all my heart.

I would also like to thank my entire family: Auntie Elaine, Auntie Janice, Auntie Phyllis and Pastor Bolls, my cousins; Philemon, Stephanis, Anthony, Omrai, Phyllis, and Phylia. My godmothers Mrs. King and Juliette (Ms. Cee Cee). To my other Mom and Dad, Bettie Payton-White and Artie Blues boy White—God placed you in my life and I love you very much. To my pastor Leroy Jones and his loving wife Sister Jones, thank you for your guidance and prayers. To Bishop Craig Bamon and his lovely wife Yvonne (also my cuz)—I love you for your prayers and your guidance. To all my friends, I love you all.

Thank you Mr. Manu Shetty for coming aboard to assist with my project.

Thank you Mr. John Lennox for your editing skills.

Mrs. Mary Cooper, words cannot express how grateful I am to you. Thank you for a job well done with the cover design, book layout, and the final edit for ***My Child, My Responsibility***.

For Mrs. Florida Williams,
Thank you for being a listener, as well as a helping hand with my project. I would like to say God has blessed me with the presence of a true friend. I have no doubt, that you are genuine and pure. Love you.

Contents

1 Origins.. 9

2 Early Adult Life.. 28

3 Marriage 36

4 What I Have Learned... 47

5 Giving Your Child Guidance and Structure............ 55

6 Some Food For Thought 66

7 School.. 67

8 Minding Your Child's Business............................... 74

9 Child Abuse 82

10 Detecting Child Abuse 87

11 Stop the Violence in Our Youth Today.................. 91

12 Reality Check.. 103

"If there is anything that we wish to change in the child, we should first examine it and see whether it is not something that could better be changed in ourselves."

~ Carl G. Jung
1939

My Child, My Responsibility Pledge

To my child I pledge to do my best as your parent.
I promise to love you,
I promise to be your guide,
I will be here with you through the ups and downs of
your everyday life, right by your side;
I won't just tell you what to do;
I know you are looking at the example I demonstrate
to you;
I will teach you morals, values, and right from wrong;
I will teach you how to stand strong;
I know you are watching, and patterning your life
after me.
I take the responsibility of my duty to be the best role
model and parent I can be.

For more information about the
My Child, My Responsibility Pledge,
and for other information regarding
Jonetta Smith's work, visit:

www.jonettasmith.com
jonetta@jonettasmith.com

CHAPTER ONE

Origins

I remember vividly how my grandfather would take our family back to Arkansas every summer in his Buick. Granny and one grandchild would sit in the front and the rest of the family—my mother, Auntie Ester, her son, John, and my brother, Jake (depending on who was in front)—would ride in the back seat. Yet we all fit comfortably in the car and there would be no arguing or quarreling ever. We were happy to be together and greatly enjoyed going to see my great grandparents. For that's where my mom met my dad, right in Arkansas. They knew each other as kids, but were not really close, although my dad lived just four houses from my great grandparents' home.

My grandfather was a man of intelligence; he was also highly educated. He served in the military and worked to provide for his family. Granddad was a man who believed that it was his responsibility to be the man of the household. To him this meant that he never raised his voice when he spoke, and he never once mistreated the women in the house. When my grandfather came home from work at the steel mill every evening (to a table already set with the meal Granny had prepared), we would have a family discussion over dinner. Then Granddad would help us with our homework. That's what I grew up seeing.

I remember when my grandfather said something, whether he was giving instructions or giving advice to one of us, we never second-guessed what he said, and we never thought of going behind his back to Granny. We could not ask Granny the same thing that we had just asked Granddad, because when a parent (or grandparent) said something to a child, it was obeyed. One could not disregard the authority of either of them. I saw that whenever my mom approached either of my grandparents with a request, before answering they would ask her whether she'd asked the other. If she had, I would hear them ask her, "What did he say?" or, "What did she tell you?" Then the final answer would be, "Well I agree with whatever your dad said," or, "I agree with your mom."

They had shared values in other ways too. Both my grandparents came from Arkansas, where they were born and raised, to Chicago. They left behind the country life so that they could live and raise their girls in the city. They both believed there would be more opportunities for them in the city to get ahead in life. Even though my grandfather never went to church with us, he respected the fact that Granny was very active there. I think that while Granddad with his life experience brought education into the family, Granny contributed God and holiness. I also think that is how today's families are different. If both parents are at home and contributing to the family, children will learn that it's important to understand what values and principles are, because they see them lived and demonstrated at home.

My grandmother was an elegant, poised woman. She respected herself not only as a woman but also as a wife and as a mother. Granny was ordained as a minister in the church. She believed that the only way to raise a child was in the eyes of God. Not only was she respected in the house; people respected Granny everywhere she went. Most people thought of her as their adopted mom. Granny was a woman of prayer: when people were sick, she prayed for them; if they were overwhelmed by the trials and tribulations of life, she prayed for them. She ministered not only to the old, but also to the young–often especially to the young. She dedicated her life to a calling in God, giving solace and succor to whoever needed it. Even those who did not believe in the church understood what she stood for, listened to her, and respected her opinion. She prayed for them to receive understanding and wisdom from God. If God gave her a word to minister to the people she obeyed God and delivered God's message to the people. She spoke with assurance and you knew she meant business. Granny was never one to talk in circles: she said what she meant and meant what she said.

My great grandparents' home in Arkansas was very inviting, full of light and life. My great grandfather worked in upholstery. He would make all kinds of furniture. I can still see him walking across the fields toward the house, returning home after selling his goods. At other times he would be singing gospel tunes and slaughtering a hog for breakfast sausage. My great grandma would cook in the kitchen with Granny and Mom helping. They cooked homemade biscuits with fresh hen eggs while we kids ran carefree in the fields, playing hop scotch or rock teacher (a similar game), jumping rope, or throwing balls around.

During these visits I was surrounded by three generations of my mother and grandmother's side of the family. Both my great grandfather and my grandfather proved themselves to be leaders, and we all followed and respected them as true men of the household. They both worked and took care of their families. They stood on the front line to protect and provide for their families. It was an honor to be in their presence. Both were men of intelligence and knowledge to spread throughout the family. Ephesians 6:4 reads,

> ***And, ye fathers provoke not your children to wrath: but bring them up in the nurture and admonition of the Lord."*** [1]

This explains my Granny's roots: how she learned to pray, who taught her to cook, and most importantly who taught her to be my grandfather's helpmate.

When in Arkansas we also visited my grandfather's mom, Great Grandma Roberta. She'd been a single parent, but her southern roots and beliefs were no different than those of my grandmother's parents. Most people from those parts believed in the concept of a village raising a child. For the most part, each neighbor was like another relative. I remember, during our visits to my great grandparents, seeing people outside with their deep fryers, cooking fish they had just caught, their music playing and the children just enjoying themselves. No gangs, no violence—just peace on the block. It was like a family reunion every weekend. As a child I really looked forward to every Friday: for on weekends I'd see the older folks like my great grandparents sitting around in their rocking chairs with their fly swatters, mosquito spray, and green rubbing alcohol in case of an insect bite—all on the lookout for every child. Humming a song they just made up as they went. Or an old hymn with the words like, "When we all get to heaven what a day of rejoicing it would be. When we all see Jesus we will sing and shout the victory."

Now there was a big difference between my mom's family and my dad's family, whom we also visited from time to time while we were down south. My dad's mom lived there, though the only times I visited her was when my mom took me to her house. My dad's mom had been a single parent like Great Grandma Roberta, but she did not seem to share Great Grandma Roberta's values. I hated to even go by her house when we visited, because of the stories I had heard about her as I was growing up. I was told that she was very mean and hateful to people. I remember how she also kept roosters and hens, and how her home smelled really bad; windows were always closed shut and the shades were drawn. No light came in and the animals ran freely all over the house.

My dad's family's beliefs were certainly different: for instance, I cannot remember a day when my dad went to church or even spoke of school. It is a wonder my mom fell for him. But she did: my mom just saw his good looks and forgot to check his values and morals. He had none: he was just a smooth talking, smell-good gorgeous man who used his looks to get what he wanted. My mom fell for the ***okey-dokey*** because she was a sheltered girl, and she believed that every person in the world was raised as she had been. Or maybe she thought she could teach him the values and morals she was taught. Little did she know she was headed into a brick wall! My grandmother would say to her, "I can look through muddy water and spot dry land." In other words, Granny could look at my dad and know he was not a good partner for my mom. Granny felt he was more advanced than my mom and he did not have the qualifications to be either a good husband or a good father. In her mind, Dad was clearly not ready for the commitment it would take to be a good husband to my mom or a good father to his children. So my grandparents fought hard to see that my mom did not become involved with him. But she continued to see him.

Dad was dealing with deep hurts. He had no father around. He was allowed to run free and wild as a child. For whatever reason, Dad didn't know how to treat a woman with respect. When his temper rose, physical and mental abuse followed.

Many times my grandparents tried to remove my mom from that situation, but my mom would get on an airplane from Chicago to Arkansas in pursuit of the love and happiness she thought she could find with my dad.

Then, in 1971, I was born, in Chicago, and by December of 1972 my parents were married and things had really begun to hit the fan. By that time my mom was pregnant with my little brother, Jake, and Dad was still being abusive to her. She might have realized that you can't change people if they don't want to change. Dad had big issues that he alone would have had to face. But my mom kept holding on.

Finally, my grandparents came to rescue her. They went to Arkansas and

gave her an ultimatum: Granddad said to her, "Give us Shun." (This was what they've called me since I was a baby.) "Let us raise her and you stay here running after a man who's eventually going to kill your crazy ass."
My mom agreed to come back to Chicago and stay with my grandparents.

Though life at my grandparents' house was more peaceful, it had its own challenges. While Mom was running crazy after my dad, Auntie Ester, Mom's middle sister, had started using drugs. She was the wild one among my grandparents' children. There's always one in every family. Auntie Ester was more like the tomboy of the household. She was very outspoken and wasn't afraid of anything. She would fight you if you did something wrong to her. A couple of times, Auntie Ester even gave my dad a few blows on the head. She would also protect my mom from my dad's beatings. Mom was not a fighter, nor did she like violence; she was scared to stand up to my dad. I used to say to myself, "if Dad had dated Auntie Ester instead, he would have hit her one time, and only one time, because Auntie Ester would have given him just what he needed—a taste of his own medicine." Dad didn't even think about starting a fight when Auntie Ester was around. Dad knew who he could push around, and who he couldn't.

Auntie Ester lived with my grandparents as well. She had a son named John. Auntie Ester met John's father in Arkansas also. John's father lived in the neighborhood where my great grandparents lived. Auntie Ester lived in Arkansas for a few years with John, but decided to move back to Chicago so my grandparents could help her with him.

Even though Auntie Ester had gotten into using drugs, she also had talent. She would sing at church. and everyone would feel her talent. She loved to sew, and she could style hair. Regardless, she kept her distance from Granny. She knew Granny would light right into her fire. Granny just took it upon herself to help with raising Jake, John, and I. Although I did try to help: because I was the oldest grandchild, when my mom enrolled me in school, I would come home and teach them everything I had learned there—their ABCs and 123s. Still, Granny had her hands full: Auntie Ester was gone for the most part, and John, the youngest of the three of us, loved to play all the time. He was very hyper: he would eat sugar from a spoon, or he would make himself syrup sandwiches. Anything sweet John could get his hands on, he would eat. He would also play so hard that he often forgot to take washroom breaks! At night Granny would have to make him go to bed.

It was Granny's duty, in fact, to keep the whole family in line. Everyone that lived inside my grandparents' home and even people who visited the household knew the limits once they stepped in. Those who lived there had daily chores. As the grandchildren became old enough we were given daily chores as well. Our chores were washing dishes, cleaning the bathroom, sweeping the kitchen, cleaning our rooms, taking out the garbage, dusting, and vacuuming. There was no discrimination: we all had to participate in the upkeep of our home. My granny gave us our routine for the week and we followed that routine, no ifs, ands, or buts. There were no favorites; we were all treated equally and we did as we were told.

I was very devoted to Granny. Wherever my granny went, I was right there with her. If she went to the bathroom, I would follow her. I would call my mother Mom and also say Mom to Granny, though at times my mother would feel like Granny was taking over her role as my parent.

When I was about three, my father showed up. He came to Chicago to be with Mom and I. You would think my mom would have said enough is enough. But guess what? She didn't! Instead, she started seeing my father again, and for at least a year they went through ups and downs. My grandparents stayed close because they knew my dad was a ticking bomb. The smallest things would send him into a rage and my mom would end up with a nosebleed or a black eye. Even though Granny could not intervene physically, I do know she prayed day in and day out for my mom. She would say, "God watches over fools and babies." Then one day, about a year after my dad showed up, Granny did intervene. My dad started to beat my mom, Granny saw it, and was not having it any longer. She put her Jesus aside, and got her shotgun and ran my dad right out of Chicago.

Now, don't get me wrong. I loved the ground my dad walked on. He would put me on his shoulders and carry me around; he'd play his music in the car while I sat in his lap as he drove. Cruising through the town in his fine car I remember people looking and saying, "That's Jerry Smith and his daughter." But as I look back, I don't believe my father had the best interests of his children at heart. The way he treated my mother affected not only her: it affected my brother and I as well. As a child I would get the feeling that we were better off without him around. It's hurtful to say, but my dad was supposed to think of his children and their well-being before anything else. And my brother deeply needed him to be the main role model for his life.

It was years before we saw our father again. He gave no child support to our mom, and offered us no mental or physical support at all.

I think not having a father hurt Jake more than it hurt me. Jake really needed fatherly guidance. He needed that main role model only a father figure can provide. When their fathers are missing, young boys tend to stray away and become influenced more by their environment. Now, looking back, I can say my brother Jake has gone through unnecessary pain as well. Once a loving little boy, he has now built up hatred for several things, the main thing being that he had no father in his life. He had no dad to play ball with him, or to teach him morals and life values. I'm sure that hurt my brother.

The only male role model Jake respected was our grandfather. Jake definitely lost his path and his direction, once our grandfather died in 1980. When he died I was nine years old. My brother was seven, my cousin John, four. We were just kids with a loving mom and loving grandparents. Before Granddad passed away we would visit the hospital to see him. John and Jake would tell Granddad to get in his wheelchair so they could run with him down the hospital corridors. Granddad loved that and so did they. That was the closest we would ever come to having a father figure in our lives.

When our grandfather passed away, Granny stepped into his place as head of the household. She knew Granddad so well, and she gave the girls the guidance, support, and great leadership that he would have given us. So later, even when we girls strayed, we still had my grandparents' beliefs, values, and leadership in our minds.

Years later, when I was ten, my dad returned with a Green Machine (a kind of Big Wheel) for me and toys for Jake. He would leave and show up later with similar gifts. Meanwhile, we kept taking annual vacations to Arkansas for family reunions. As Jake and I grew older we would walk around Arkansas looking for our dad. We felt that at any time he might drive up that rocky road to our great grandparents' house in a fine car.

Although he and my mom were still legally married, Dad had started his own life with other women and repeated the same pattern of violence with them. My mom later learned that he had other children: a daughter, older than me, that he never claimed, and another girl the same age as Jake. To this day I have never met my older sister. I know she lives in Arkansas, but that's about all I know. My half-sister, Toya, and I met once when we were teenagers. But it would be years before we spoke or met again.

As a single parent my mom worked and went to school to support my brother and I. With the support of her parents she was able to continue her education and get several degrees in school. She became a pharmacist. Mom did her best to commit to the terms of ***My Child, My Responsibility***. At times she was maybe too trusting of others: she befriended lots of people, which was good and bad. But despite what she went through, I believe she did her best for her children.

She was helped by the example of her sisters. Case in point: Auntie Caroline, who was a great figure in my life too. I would go stay with her and her husband for about two weeks during my summer break. She was the spitting image of Granny. Auntie Caroline was strict but fun at the same time. You knew how far you could push the envelope with her. She had rules in her household, and it was like boot camp in a sense, but it was still inviting. She ran her household on a schedule: when you get up in the morning, you wash your face, brush your teeth, make your bed, and then prepare for breakfast. Her routine went throughout the entire day.

My Auntie Caroline's strength allowed her to become a woman of great leadership. She now has her master's in child education; she also became a minister, like my granny, and the mother of two boys. To this day Auntie Caroline still attends school, saying always, "You can never learn enough."

The baby girl of Mom's generation of the family was Auntie Anna, and she was just that: a big baby. She's ten years younger than my mom: when my mom went shopping for me she would buy Auntie Anna gifts as well. Auntie Anna would only come out of her room to go to school, have dinner, do her homework, and chores. After that she was right back in her room. But Auntie Anna always had time to help my mom comb my hair, and keep me looking pretty.

Auntie Anna married at a young age: she was in her early twenties. She met her husband in a lounge—a place my grandmother would never have imagined my Auntie Anna visiting. Worse than that, the man had already been married and had children. Of course my grandparents—this was shortly before my grandfather died—did not approve, and the entire family was devastated when she went to city hall and got married. But it worked out for

Auntie Anna and her husband; they have been married for twenty-five years and have had their own church for almost fourteen years now; both are ministers. My uncle had two children from his previous marriage and they have a family of four children together.

This was indeed a very surprising change for my uncle. Growing up, he almost never attended church. But one Sunday, hearing how my Auntie Anna was raised there, he decided to attend church with the family. From that day on he has not missed a day of church service.

Later I heard my Auntie Anna was talking at the club about how my grandparents raised her. Only Auntie Anna would bring church talk into the club. The apple might fall from the tree, but not too far. Even when she felt like getting out of line, what my grandparents taught her always stayed with her.

Granny, though, was the best example for my mom. I never heard my granny use profanity, and I never saw her drink, smoke, wear pants, or even dance, unless she was doing the Holy Ghost dance in church.

She led by her example and expected nothing less than what she gave us. My grandfather did smoke and drink, but looking back now I don't remember him ever smoking or drinking in the house. Granddad would sit out on the front porch every morning drinking coffee and that's where he would smoke his cigarettes. Granddad had a high level of respect for my granny; whatever he did in the streets stayed in the streets. I heard he would go out with his friends from work and have a few drinks. But never would he allow his friends to drink in his home around his family.

As they grew older, however, my mom and aunties wanted to do other things besides attend church all week long. They wanted to do things they really never got a chance to do as teenagers. They really didn't socialize with their friends at school, go to parties, or wear pants. My mom and her sisters had grown up, and though they were still respectful of my grandparents, they wanted to do things they knew Granny would not approve of.

Mom wanted to be independent and she wanted to have her male company visit her at home. In my grandparents' home her male company could visit, but they couldn't go further than the living room. If it wasn't pleasing in God's eyes, Granny believed, then it didn't belong in her house. My mom wanting to be free to do things she knew my granny wouldn't have in her home, she decided it was time to move out of her parents' home. And that's just what she did.

When she left for Iowa, Jake went with her; I wanted to live with my grandparents. And I stayed right there until I finished eighth grade. My mom had tried to get me to move with her when she relocated to Iowa, but I wasn't thinking about moving nowhere my granny wasn't. So during the summer after I finished sixth grade, my mom tricked me, saying, "Just come to Iowa for the summer." I agreed to go, and as summer was ending I asked when I would be going back to Chicago. My mom said, "You won't be leaving. You are my child and you will go to school here in Iowa."

I think I only stayed there three months of the school year. Sure, I felt comfortable. I met some nice people there. I became very close with a girl named Melba. I got to do things Granny would not approve of. We would ride her mopeds around town and I would spend the night at her house. Spending the night over at a friend's house was not something Granny allowed me to do. Especially if they had older brothers.

I went along with her program for a while, but soon my mom had moved a man in with us. I wasn't receptive to him at all from the beginning. My brother and I shared a room together. I started to think about protecting the two of us: every night I would sleep with a hammer under my pillow because I had heard things about Mom's boyfriend that were not so pleasant. One day I came home to find him lying naked on the living room floor. My mom said that he had taken sick. She told me that because she knew if I had any idea her boyfriend was using drugs I would go back to Chicago without any hesitation. But I said enough is enough: she had already tricked me into going out there for the summer, which turned into me staying for school. And now this?

Maybe he wasn't as bad as I was told, or maybe he was. But as a child I thought that it wasn't a good thing for me to see my mom's boyfriend laid out sick or high on drugs. I shouldn't have been placed in such a situation. I was just a child and though things might have been worse, I was raised by my grandparents to believe that if something didn't feel comfortable to me then it wasn't right.

I went to a friend's house and used their phone to call Granny. I told Granny to come get me. By the nightfall she'd sent her troops out to get me. Auntie Ester, her boyfriend Will, and Mom's god brother—my uncle Joe—had arrived in Iowa. Mom was shocked because she had no idea they were coming. I had secretly packed my clothes in a trash bag and was ready to go.

My Aunt Ester put my bags in the car and then told my mom to get her stuff too. It was time for her to leave as well. By then Mom's boyfriend came running out of the house trying to prevent her from leaving. Auntie Ester wasn't leaving without Mom. She told her: "Look here, we don't want any problems out of you. Get yourself in this car and let's roll." But Mom's boyfriend insisted on getting in the car with us.

My aunt agreed to have him come with us back to Chicago—or so Mom thought. But really Auntie Ester had a different plan in mind. She knew the only way my mom would agree to get in the car is if she thought her boyfriend was coming with her. My aunt started to drive toward the highway that would take us back to Chicago, but suddenly she took a turn, and after a short detour we all found ourselves sitting in front of a police station. That is where my aunt requested that my mom's boyfriend get out of the car, and then she pulled away, leaving him in front of the police station.

All the way back to Chicago Mom was crying, having a fit. She thought we had a good life in Iowa, but I don't know how she could have really believed that. I know she wanted to be independent and on her own with her children. That would have been fine. But I had one problem: it wasn't just Mom and her children. It was someone else as well. I felt she should have dated her boyfriend, but he should not have moved in with us. He should have lived where he was while the three of us lived in our own house. Especially since Mom was the only one providing for the household. I looked at Mom's boyfriend as someone who had no intention of helping her with the family financially or emotionally. When we returned to Chicago I lived with Granny until my junior year in high school. My mom moved with Jake not far from my grandparents' home.

Things changed when I became a teenager. After my junior year in school I knew if I went to stay with my mom she would allow me to go to my senior prom, so I moved back in with her. Things Granny disapproved of I knew Mom would allow me to do. Prom was something I really wanted to attend and Granny was not going to allow me to. Granny's church would host an event for the seniors graduating high school. But there were only two of us from school that belonged to Granny's church and would come, and of course senior prom with all the rest of my high school classmates sounded much more fun. As far as me dating, going out with the kids from school, and participating in school activities, Granny didn't allow any of these. She had strict rules: she wanted me to get my education, enjoy my life as a teenager, and hang out with the church kids. There would be absolutely no sex before marriage. I didn't even wear pants around Granny until about the age of sixteen, afraid of what she would think I had become.

I was taught that if I had something I wanted to say to my mom or to Granny I could say it, as long as I was respectful when expressing my feelings. So I didn't hesitate to tell my mom when I became sexually active, and I told her that she should tell Granny. But to my surprise, Granny already knew! She had seen me starting to change and she could tell when I began having sex. Little did I know she still kept close a watch on me!

Once, when I was a teenager and felt I needed privacy in my grandparents' home, I placed a "Do Not Enter" sign in big bold letters on my bedroom door. My grandparents, however, told me politely that the sign had to come down. When I got my own home, they said, I could place it wherever I liked—as long as it was in my own home. They told me that instead I should hang a sign that read "You Are Welcome to Enter at All Times." They also said that my door could be closed when necessary, but for the most part it was to remain open—even when I wanted to have a private conversation with a boy I liked, or I had juicy gossip to talk about privately with my friends.

My granny was all up in my biz, as we used to say. She kept watch on me to make sure I wasn't persuaded or easily influenced by my friends. "Don't let your friends get you in trouble," she would say. She would decide who I should and should not have as friends. "Some girls are fast tail girls," she'd say, "and I don't want you caught playing with them." I would tell myself, Granny just doesn't understand. But truth be told, Granny understood perfectly: her main concern was her grandchild. She didn't want me to become mixed up with the wrong crowd. She'd say, "I didn't want someone to snatch you off where I can't find you." That was her main concern and she let me know that constantly. She would tell me not to talk to strangers, to stay with the crowd when coming home from school. I would hear those words every day when leaving home. Granny would watch the news every night, and she would see how children went missing, or how someone was killed. She would then say, "When the street lights come on, you should be sitting on this porch.

Do not let me have to come looking for you." I would know exactly want she meant because if she came looking for me, she wouldn't be alone. Granny would have a switch that she had cut from our backyard tree. Even after I had become an adult, until the day my granny died, she would call me on the phone to tell me what she saw on the news, and to remind me to be careful going in and out my home. I would say, "Okay, yes ma'am, Granny," and she would reply, "Take heed to what I am saying. You never too grown to listen."

At that time, though, I thought this was too strict. I was a teenager and wanted to hang out. I saw my friends hanging out after the streetlights came on and asked, why can't I too? I tried very hard not to be disobedient, but sometimes I would try to push the envelope. To my surprise, I couldn't push the envelope too far with Granny. She was on it every time I tried to get past her. She would say, "You got to rise early to fool me and I rise mighty early."

Yes, Granny was strict. The only porch I could sit on after the street lights came on was my godparents'. They lived two doors down from Granny. Poppa and Mama King's home was the only place I could go without Granny feeling she had to watch over me. My godparents had children of their own who grew up with my mom and her siblings. So Poppa and Mama King treated me like one of their own. They were part of my community and took an interest in it. Another of Granny's rules was that I wasn't allowed to be present during grown folks' conversation. When I received a look from her, I knew to remove myself.

I recall ditching math class in high school one day. Instead I went to music. There I was very surprised to hear the news: Shun's grandmother was in the building. It had traveled fast all over the school, but when it reached me it was too late: right in front of the class I was slapped by my granny and escorted back to my math.

It was the wake-up call I needed: after that incident Granny never had to come again to my high school. I went on to finally complete my education, attending summer school, night classes, and finally finishing with a home program.

Meanwhile, Mom was on her third child. Mom met my baby sister Jasmine's dad in Iowa as well. He was not involved in Jasmine's childhood, and to this day she rarely hears from him. I think Mom didn't believe in herself. She didn't think she could be the strong woman that God created her to be. She was entirely too trusting of people and thought that everyone that came into her life had good intentions.

Her difficulties grew: while my brother Jake, now a teenager, developed a negative attitude toward life and started giving her trouble, Mom still had baby sis, my cousin John, and me to deal with. You might as well say John was Mom's child too. Whenever we moved, John came with. He had no other children to be with besides Jake and I, so it felt natural to always have him around. Since Jasmine and I are fourteen years apart, I began to help Mom raise her. I would comb her hair, give her baths, and take her wherever I went as if she was my own baby. My mom could not really comb hair. When I was growing up as a little girl my aunties would comb my hair. So I knew to help Mom out with keeping my little sister dressed like a little doll. And that's exactly how I looked at Jasmine—as a little doll. She was so precious and innocent that giving her tender loving care was the natural thing to do: so I'd been taught when I was a little girl.

So while I was placed on the right path when I became a teenager, my brother grew rebellious and disobedient toward both my mom and Granny. With our grandfather deceased and our father not present in his life at all, Jake just wanted to hang out with his friends. Even at the age of thirteen he was turning into this uncontrollable character. To this day, Jake has spent more time in jail than outside it. When he's in jail he becomes a changed man: he writes to the family about how he has changed his life, how he will be on the right path when he comes home. But Jake is now in his thirties, and is singing the same song. The only person that is losing sleep and peace of mind over his situation is my mom. She worries all the time; she is always upset and crying about Jake's situation. It is a sad thing to say, but when my brother is in jail, Mom is able to get some rest: she doesn't need to worry about him being on the streets every night searching for his next fix. We hear so much about loved ones being found dead somewhere in the streets as a result of using drugs. When Jake is in jail, Mom doesn't need to imagine him not returning home.

Once Jake comes home from jail, he goes right back to his same ways: using drugs and destroying his life. He feels the world owes him something. Everything that has happened in his life is someone else's fault; he never takes responsibility for his own actions. Jake expects a big celebration every time he is released from jail. He wants people to give him money, clothes, and a car. The first time he came home I was all for celebrating his return, hoping to see a changed man, someone who has realized that the life he has chosen keeps him in bondage. By the time he was on his third release from jail I started to say to my mom: "Hold on, we are spending our hard-earned money celebrating what? Jake returning home? Jake changing his life? He's not returning home from the military or on spring break from college. He's returning home from jail, a place he should not have gone to in the first place!"

I feel Jake needs to show himself love. Only he can change the life he is living. The more he lies to himself, the more he destroys the chance of becoming the great person he could really become. To this day I tell my mom to stop thinking of what she did wrong with him. I tell her not to allow Jake to manipulate her as a parent. She had to be both mom and dad to all of us, and she did her best. But it's up to us now to learn from our past, to move beyond it. Turn Jake over to God, I say, and focus on my baby sister and yourself. Tough love is what Jake needs.

CHAPTER TWO

Early Adult Life

By the time I was eighteen I was enrolled in school and training in electrocardiology (EKG) and phlebotomy. I wanted to become a pediatrician. Around that time I also got a job at the Water Tower in downtown Chicago. It was a fun learning experience for me. My mom did not have to tell me to get a job. I wanted to help mom take care of my little sister and to have my own money. Growing up in my household I was taught that to get what you want in life you must earn it. I would take the suburban Pace bus to downtown Chicago by myself. I learned to take public transportation to work so that I could save money to have nice things.

One day, while coming home from school, I met a young man standing outside the corner store near my house. He was passing out money to all the little children who went into the store. He gave me twenty dollars and said, "Go buy what you came for in the store." I was shocked to see someone in the neighborhood take time to help out his community. When I came out of the store he introduced himself as Mark and we exchanged numbers.

Eventually we started to date. Mark did the most romantic things for me: he brought me flowers every other day; and he took me to dinner all the time. We spent quality time together every day. When later I took a job at a bank near our home, Mark would pick me up from school and take me to work. He was such a gentlemen and everyone in my family embraced him, including Granny. My entire family being fond of Mark was really a good sign for me. Mark was very intelligent, and had a business mind. As the relationship continued my feelings grew strong for him. He dressed mostly in business attire. One day I asked him, "What is it that you do for work?" He replied, "I'm in school and I'm in sales." That seemed a little odd to me because Mark was practically at my beck and call. I thought no more about that conversation, and we continued our relationship. Though I still wasn't sure what he did to earn a living. I knew only that he kept a lot of money, he drove a few nice cars, and he would take me shopping a lot. He always told me I should dress nice going to work.

At the time I had a girlfriend, Jan, whom I'd known for about a year. She'd dated my god brother for a while, and there were rumors that she'd given him a sexually transmitted disease. But calling myself a true friend, I overlooked the fact that she was promiscuous. This trait—focusing on the good in people—I received from my mom. Jan was an only child and I knew she was having problems with her dad. When her dad spoke to her, she never really seemed to hear what he said. I noticed she would ignore him while he talked and she would talk back to him when he tried to discipline her. But I can definitely say she had a good life with him. She had her own car by the time she was a senior in high school, and she got just about everything she asked for. Jan's mom was deceased, and I think her dad felt guilty about it and spoiled her. He never really enforced discipline with her: he would point out things he did not approve of, but he never acted on his words. That is, until the summer of 1990, when he booted her out. She needed a place to stay; I asked Mom if it would be okay for her to come stay with us for a while. Mom agreed.

Jan moved in with my family and me. I introduced her to Mark when he came by one day. She instantly said she didn't like him. When I asked her how she could decide that without even knowing him, she said he was not my type. I thought that was strange: how could she tell me what was and what wasn't my type?

It did not take long to figure out why Jan did not like Mark for me: she liked him for herself.

It was the Fourth of July and Jan claimed she would catch the bus to her dad's home for the holiday. That seemed strange because she never took the bus before. Usually, Mark and I dropped her off at her dad's. I called Mark to see where he was, because he and I were supposed to go over to meet our family and friends. He didn't answer, so I walked around the corner to his mom's house to find him. I found him all right, on his mom's porch, with Jan, who was sitting on his lap.

I had dated this guy for a year without a clue as to his intentions. Later I learned Mark and Jan would sneak out with each other while I was at work, each giving me different stories as to what they were doing. But in reality they were together and secretly cheating behind my back.

That was a hard situation to deal with, learning that not only had my boyfriend betrayed me, but just as bad, I had also been betrayed by my supposed best friend. On top of that, I found out I was pregnant with Mark's child. Mark denied to my face that he could even have children. Now here I was, twenty and pregnant. I was just starting my whole career, and I wanted to pursue the dreams that I hoped for, as I was becoming a young lady. Clearly my priorities got mixed up when I started loving someone before pursuing the goals I had planned for myself. Clearly I wasn't ready to become a mom. But the child did not ask to be born. I also realized I had to make the decision to have a child, since I did nothing to prevent the pregnancy: If I did willingly what it took to conceive this child, it was now my responsibility to step up as this child's parent.

I made the choice to keep my child, whether Mark was a willing participant or not. He was an adult and a willing participant in this matter, and he would have to live with the decisions he made.

I knew this would be a life-changing decision for me, but I felt I was strong enough to make it. Otherwise, everything that my grandparents and my mother had taught me would be in vain. They would be disappointed for a while, but they would certainly be on board to support me through this major life change. It was my decision to grow up faster than my time, to disobey my elders, to ignore what they'd taught me. We as children think we know it all, but really we don't know anything. We get a taste of the real world and think we are ready for society at a young age. We reach a certain age like eighteen and think we are grown. We look forward to our eighteenth birthday because we think that means doing and saying what we want. That's exactly why I felt grown up. But the truth is we have more to learn than we could ever imagine. The real world doesn't allow the mistakes our parents do.

It wasn't Mark's fault: it was up to me to remember what my parents had taught me. Instead of disciplining me, my mom wanted to be more of a friend to me. I think she felt if she objected I would not like her, or maybe I would rebel against her. But she should have realized that she was the parent and I was the child.

That being said, both Mom and Granny shifted gears and stood right by my side. Granny went from saying to me, "You are a single young lady," to saying, "Now you have not only yourself to think about, but you are responsible for this child's life as well." No more room for play anymore; pull it all together for the little one as well. Granny supported me and became the voice in my ear telling me to do the right thing for my child. She knew being pregnant without the child's father would be difficult. Granny accompanied me to childbirth classes and doctor's appointments. Even though I was living with my mom, Granny kept visiting and continued to be the backbone of our family.

It was New Year's Eve and Granny was in church. I called her to come get me: the baby was coming. She left church and came immediately to take me to the hospital. While I kept screaming, Granny looked at me and said, "Stop the noise! Stop that yelling! Get yourself together. You are about to give birth!" Instantly I shut my mouth and focused on my granny's voice.

On New Year's morning, I delivered an 8 pound, 14 ounce baby boy. He had all his fingers and toes and he was looking around as if wondering, "Where am I?" At that time I knew my responsibilities had just begun. It was no longer just me; I had to accept responsibility for another human being. It was something I clearly wasn't prepared for. That's a prime example of the consequences of not listening to your parents. You jump, but the world that you jump into takes control, and you must be mentally equipped and prepared to deal with it. That was just the beginning of my dealing with the problems of the real world. I wanted to be grown up, but the world had other plans waiting for me.

Six months into Javonte's life in this world I noticed something wrong with his left eye. Something looked very strange. Looking at it brought tears to my eyes. I said to Mom, "Something's wrong with Vonte's eye." I made the appointment, and my mom and I first took Javonte to his primary doctor, who advised me to take him to an Ophthalmologist. I did, and she examined his eyes and advised that I take him to the hospital, since something indeed looked wrong.

So Mom, Granny and I took my baby to Children's Memorial Hospital where he was tested by Dr.. Greenwald. The result was shocking: my baby had retinoblastoma in his eye. A cancerous tumor covered his entire eyeball. Dr. Greenwald suggested he perform surgery within five days. I said, "Okay, but let me get a second opinion." I took my son to the University of Chicago and the diagnosis was the same.

I immediately told my granny to pray: they just diagnosed Vonte with cancer in his eye. I called Mark as the doctors wanted to know the history of both parents. Mark refused to cooperate. He refused, even though this was his flesh and blood. I overlooked Mark's reactions and focused on the issue at hand—my child. Pray and let God deal with fools, I thought.

Knowing that this surgery was one of the most important decisions I would have to make as an adult and as a single parent, I took my son to the church and let them pray for him.

The night before Vonte's surgery Granny called and said "I don't think you should allow the doctors to operate."

My words were: "Granny, if we don't, Vonte will suffer from cancer and his face can become disfigured. Not only that, the cancer will spread."

Granny still told me not to let them proceed. I told her to pray for a recovery and not to look for tragedy. I had to make a conscious decision on behalf of Vonte as his parent.

The next day my mom and Granny accompanied us to the hospital and the surgery went as planned. It took all morning. Once again Granny prayed for Vonte. While Vonte was in surgery Granny developed a headache—I think just because she was so worried all that time. Around one o'clock the doctor came out to tell us that the surgery went well and that Vonte was in recovery.

When Vonte finally came through the doors I almost passed out—his face was covered in bandages and a white knitted cap was over his face. Even in the midst of all that, I was grateful my child was alive and healthy. It took some time for me to get used to the fact that my son could see with only one of his eyes. But yet he was well and began to participate in life as if nothing had ever happened. I received strength from my child; he would play with other children without a worry. He would do normal things as if he never had the surgery.

It was required of me as a parent to be there to take charge, to care for my child. I created him through God. Even through the ups and downs, I was determined to not follow in my mom's footsteps. I was determined to break the cycle that haunted our family. I decided not to date or let anything else sidetrack me for almost two years. I needed to play catch-up with my education and I needed to focus on Javonte's schedule. I came home from work, helped Javonte with his learning skills, and then we both would eat the dinner Mom had cooked. I wouldn't leave my room until the next day to continue that same routine.

Mom was working on and off; she would help with Vonte every chance she would get. I gained focus in my life, and concentrated on what was best for Vonte and I. I took a job at a video store a few blocks from my house; I worked five days a week, and had weekends off. Vonte's doctor appointments and work was my routine day after day; school took the back seat.

At least once a week I would travel for almost two hours on the bus, Vonte in my arms, going from the south suburbs to the doctor's office downtown Chicago. I worked and saved money because I needed a car to take Vonte back and forth to the doctor. He was a big baby, and he was getting too heavy for me to carry on my hips.

Once I had saved enough money I went to the car lot by myself to look for a used car. After the salesman ran my credit, he told me: "You need a co-signer." I remember it like yesterday—I called my granny for her help once again. Without hesitation she came to my aid. No long discussion ensued about her co-signing for my car. Granny had felt I needed a car from the time Vonte had taken sick, but she never expressed it to me. Basically, she wanted to see how responsible I had become. That is, if I really wanted a car I would save my own money first, before asking someone to buy it for me. Granny was proud to see I had taken the first step toward making a commitment to get what was needed for Vonte and me. Not only did I get a car, I got a brand new one off the showroom floor.

After I got home with the car, Granny said these words to me. "As long as you do right and want something in life I'm here for you. Don't you forget your responsibility and stop paying that car note. If that car note is one payment late you can never ask me for anything else." She trusted that I was mature enough to know what it meant asking her to sign her name on the dotted line. That also made me aware that if she had faith in me, I should have faith in myself. I was capable of achieving whatever I wanted if only I worked for it and kept a positive attitude toward myself. As Granny and Mom were positive toward me, I kept their words in my mind, and so far I've achieved everything I started out to do, often without even a thought of deviating from my plans.

CHAPTER THREE

Marriage

Later, I worked at the municipal building in the south suburbs of Chicago in the accounts and finance department. A man named Mr. Gino would come to city hall to receive payment for the work he had done for the city. When he came, Mr. Gino would always make it his business to speak to me. One day while waiting he got up the courage to invite me out for dinner. I accepted his invitation, not thinking that two years later he would become my husband. He was twelve years my senior and he had been married once before and had one child from that marriage. Knowing Vonte needed a man in his life, I was pleased to see that Gino stepped up and began to fit the profile of a good dad. They played ball, went fishing, and did all the activities father and son would do together. One day, out of the blue, Vonte called Gino Dad. We looked at each other and let well enough alone. Vonte was only two and had never met his father. Vonte just assumed calling Gino dad was the appropriate thing to do. As the year ended we learned I was pregnant.

We started to look for a home to rent so that we could be together as a family. Twenty-four years old with one child and one on the way, I still had to make sure my finances were right. So I worked throughout the entire pregnancy. As self-sufficient parents with morals, we were obligated to make sure the family survived the odds. I still felt my life was incomplete. Once before, I had put school at the end of my list because of Vonte's illness. Gino would say, "You should go back to school and finish your education." Gino was somewhat like my grandfather: he had completed college and also gone into the military. Education was very important to him. There was nothing Gino would not try to fix, make, or put together. He was a whiz: he was the man who would fix something himself before paying someone else to do it. He instilled hard work in our children early.

In the summer of 1995 Gino Jr. was born. I returned to work two months later, and I returned to the same routine. But now I had two children to get ready, take to day care, and come home to cook dinner for. But I loved it and thought we were living the American dream.

It was important for the family to do fun things together every weekend. Gino was very active with teaching and showing the children different things in the world. On many Sunday afternoons Gino would say, "Let's take a ride with the children." We would also travel with our children. Every time we took a family trip I would also include my little sister, Jasmine. I wanted her to experience things the children and I were experiencing. We would drive to Wisconsin just to look at the trees and see the difference between the winter and spring foliage. I never really appreciated the leaves on the trees or paid attention to the change in their coloring until I met Gino. As a young teenager he had been on several vacations that he thought he should revisit with us as a family. His entire family would go on trips every year when he was growing up. Gino had no fear about packing our bags and heading to a different state or city—Disney World, the Wisconsin Dells, Ohio or Arkansas for a family reunion. The kids loved to camp as well. Personally, when we went camping, I just went along to support the family. I didn't like sleeping on the ground, and I definitely did not like the flying insects, the bugs. But I went to experience a different atmosphere. As long as the boys and Gino were having fun I tagged along to be a sport. Having been in the military as a marine, Gino had a wealth of outdoors knowledge and could teach our children how to survive in this world.

The American dream lasted about two years, and then I discovered that Mr. Gino was cheating on me. He was running around with some co-worker at his job. Here I am with a four-year-old and a two-month-old baby and this guy has the nerve this early in the game to cheat on the family. We started to argue, and this little fairy tale quickly turned into reality. After so many arguments I packed his belongings and asked him to leave.

We were separated for about a week: he went to his mom's house and I stayed home with the kids. It was our first major disagreement. I clearly wasn't ready to just say it's over with our relationship. I started to have thoughts of me having two children with no father figure present. This was something I had already experienced with Mark, and I clearly was not about to end the relationship that easily. I started to think: I will not let this other woman disrupt our home. Many reasons why I should not end the relationship came to my mind. But very few reasons came as to why I should end it. It was a difficult situation that was on my mind, and I was considering the wrong reasons. Both of us believed we were about to lose one another, but the topic of what was best for the children never came up. We thought only of what we wanted for ourselves.

After things cooled off Gino returned home and we decided to give our relationship another try. I looked at our relationship differently from that point on. Now it was always in the back of my mind that he was capable of hurting me mentally, and I also learned to put my guard up in case he felt the urge to cheat again. As if that wasn't enough, I also learned later that he had two other children, something I thought he should have told me at the beginning of our relationship. I asked him, "What is the big secret about not telling me how many children you have?" Then I discovered the reason he didn't tell me. When his first child was born, Gino was too young to care for the baby and the girl's aunt raised the baby. As for the second child, he had cheated on his first wife and the woman he had cheated with became pregnant. Yet, knowing all that, I still decided to marry Gino anyway. In 1996 we got married and soon afterward our daughter Princess was born.

I went on to further my education in child development so that I could open my own daycare center. I was now twenty-seven years old with three children. As I was a mother of three children, my granny would come to my home and take care of my children in the evenings when I worked late. Not only was she there to help me out, she was there to help Gino out too. He too worked long hours and deserved a cooked meal after working so hard. He and I would come home to a cooked dinner that Granny had prepared for the entire family. So we gave thanks and came together. When I entered my home it felt warm and welcoming, and Granny would be asleep in Gino's chair with our baby daughter in her arms. How many grandmothers today really take time with their own grandchildren or great grandchildren?

Whatever I decided to do my grandmother supported it. Even when I made a bad choice, she gave her opinion about the matter, but left the decision in my hands. Many things that occurred in my life were not planned or even talked about beforehand. But when something happened in my life I accepted it, and just put my mind in gear to work it out, knowing that whatever affects me will also affect my children. As a child I had heard about the struggle and sacrifice my grandparents and great grandparents had made. Each generation suffered to provide stability for the next. I believe it was their goal for us not to turn right around and repeat the same patterns they had, but to learn from their struggles. Now, as I look back I realize what the message was for me. The message was: "Think before you make life-changing decisions. The decisions you make become your present and determine your future."

It took me until Vonte was about six years old for me to realize that my choices affect my children too. It had gotten to the point where Gino and I would argue and he would take his anger out on Vonte. I began to see the change in their relationship after Little Gino was about three years old. His father would take him fishing or wherever he was going and Vonte would be left at home with me. Not only did I notice it; Vonte noticed it too. Vonte would ask, "Can I come too?" And Gino's reply would be, "You stay here with your mom." Gino started to say things like that to Vonte more often. My family also noticed the change. One day my brother approached Gino and told him, "I see you showing favor between Vonte and Little Gino. Do not mistreat my nephew."

Our marriage was definitely taking a turn for the worse. I hated when Gino called me names. ***Bitch*** was his favorite word. He used that word often and that made me feel hostile toward him. My life was in constant turmoil; I was not happy and felt Vonte was not happy as well. Never did I imagine we would become so vicious toward one another. But we did. Once, while we were having an argument, Gino put his hands around my throat. I freed myself, called the police, and had him removed from our property. That was the beginning of the end. I knew in my heart I wasn't going to take any physical abuse: I had children to take care of. I had young boys who would soon become young men. I didn't want my daughter to think it was okay to allow any man to put his hands on her. We can argue and have disagreements all day long, but when it becomes physical it's time for one of us to pack up and go.

Both of us let our marriage get far beyond reconcilable. Our arguments were way out of control. It was clear we needed guidance from someone who could help us calm things down. Neither of us wanted to admit we were wrong; the picture in his mind made him right, and the picture in my mind made me right. There was no compromising, no middle ground for either of us. Did we think to sit down and work out our problems? No, not at all. It was all talk and no action. At this point, without God's grace or even counseling our marriage was certain to dissolve. Did we think about the children in the midst of our arguing? Did we think that our actions would also affect their lives as well? The children watched us argue, and a few times it even got to the point where we physically fought in front of them. I was just ready to run away and not look back. That would have been selfish. I got into this marriage because that was what I wanted. Now I'm getting out of the marriage and relationship of nine years because that's what I want too. Gino really didn't want a divorce, so he ignored the court dates. I thought that divorce was a solution that would bring closure to the relationship now that it had turned so hateful between us. We both forgot the most important issue: the children also travel in our journey with us. Lesson well learned!

It is hard not having your parents together under the same roof. So we as parents need to realize when we divorce that the children experience the consequences of the divorce too. They feel they shouldn't have to say who was right or who was wrong in your marriage; they should not be placed in a situation where they have to choose between parents. We as parents are so wrong for involving children in our dysfunctional relationships. During the divorce, we have hateful and spiteful thoughts about our partner. We don't realize that this is not a time for thinking only of victory. Why? Because you both have lost your battle in marriage. The vows you took have sat on the back burner. It has become an issue of what each of you want, or what each of you think you deserve. Even the children become a target in the divorce process. They become a dollar sign; they become objects of custody battles, and begin to be pulled between parents. Divorce, I admit, is a lot of pressure for an adult. What makes you think the child can deal with the pressure of a divorce battle, if we as adults become overwhelmed? I say to you, they can't and should not be asked to deal with it. Express the love you both share for the children, assure the children you are still there to listen, to help them become strong through a terrible situation that we as parents have placed them in.

Once you start the divorce process you and your ex-spouse really should have a civil conversation about the kids. The major topics should be emotional and financial support for the children. Child support is important. But what if one loses a job? Your children will someday go to college—at least that is what we hope. Who will be responsible for life insurance for the children? How many days in a week will the absent parent call and talk to the children? I also believe that there should be a law stating that whichever spouse is ordered to pay child support, and for whatever reason they stop paying, the law would order them to take out some type of insurance policy, if the arrears are greater than $5,000. There should be an order to get a life insurance policy. Because one out of three child support cases end up un-paid and the arrears remain.

Now that I'm divorced I speak with my children every day to see what's on their mind and what could be done to include them in my daily thought process. Vonte is now a senior in high school. I have received several e-mails from his English teacher informing me of his status. When he gets home I pull out my cell phone and show him—you missed class today. As Vonte starts to grab on to manhood he wants to challenge me a little more. He came home drunk one time. That night, I went and got a bottle of vodka from the cabinet and gave it to him and said, "Drink." All he wanted to do was hold the toilet. Guess what? I left him right there all night. He hardly had time to speak to me, he was so busy throwing his guts up, but his look said it all: "Lady are you crazy?" It was a point I wanted to prove to him. Don't put your lips on nothing you have no idea about. It was not time to baby him. He felt he wanted to step into grown folk shoes, so I treated the situation like an adult situation. Still knowing that he was a child, but making him aware of just that—you are still a child. Since that day we have not had any other problems with alcoholic beverages.

Little Gino was always more challenging, even from the time he could walk and talk. One day, when I went to pick the children up from the sitter, I placed Little Gino in the car first, and then I went back to the sitter's door to get Princess. Little Gino, at the age of three decides he wants to drive! He put the car in drive and hid under the steering wheel. The car headed into the neighbor's gate about five houses from the babysitter's place. Thank God no damage was done. When I got into the car I found Little Gino crying, saying, "Mommy, I want to drive just like you."

One day, when Vonte was nine and Little Gino was six, I received a phone call from the local police station telling me that my sons and three of their friends were in custody. They were caught in a movie store putting movies in their pockets. The boys were supposed to be riding bikes with their friends and ended up over five miles away from home in a video store, stealing. Both of them knew right from wrong: the police officer told me that Little Gino had begged them not to call his mom because she worked for the police station as well.

When I picked them up from the police station they expected to be punished, but they had no idea what the punishment would be. I gave each of them a Bible, made them stand holding the book above their heads for about fifteen minutes until they realized what they did was wrong. I also changed the company they kept—some of those boys were eleven and twelve years old and had no parental guidance at home.

When Little Gino completed elementary school, his father was living in Nashville, and we talked about letting Little Gino go live with him there. I agreed because I knew that would be best for Little Gino. He needed his father in his life and, as I mentioned earlier, Gino had a college degree and could teach his son the things he knew. Especially now, since Little Gino was interested in sports. He wanted to play football and his dad wanted to help him in the transition to adolescence. As much as we disagreed about what happened in our marriage, Gino Sr. tried to stay on board with Little Gino and Princess emotionally. But financially, Gino would fall behind in child support as he moved from job to job.

Ms. Princess, the baby of our family, is daddy's baby. She took the divorce really hard, started to show her emotions through eating, and gained weight. As she grasped the word "divorce" she realized our family would no longer be the same at home. She thought we did nothing to save the marriage. I learned later on she believed we should have tried to make it work. She said that all parents cheat and have up and downs. Looking in her eyes, I could tell she and her friends discussed their parent's lifestyles, regardless of whether they were single, married, or divorced. That's when I opened up to her and explained that you can't let anyone mistreat you: you don't have to accept mental or physical abuse from anyone. I stood firm on my words to her. I also explained it was not her fault that her dad and I couldn't work it out.

Princess decided she wanted to be the class clown in the school. She walked out of several classes thinking she didn't have to participate. This behavior came so suddenly with Princess, and we weren't sure why. Maybe she was feeling defeated by her lesson. Maybe she felt too proud to ask her teachers to repeat something. Or maybe she felt too embarrassed to say she didn't understand. One day, I received a call from the principal of the school to say the entire school staff was looking for Princess. I went to the school and when I arrived she was in the principal's office crying. I immediately made a conference call to her dad. It was important that I include him in this, even though he was in Tennessee; his voice has a great impact on Princess. She tends to get her act together just a little bit faster when he's around. I knew it was critical to put a plan in place for her with her schoolwork.

As a parent I feel defeated if my child feels defeated; it was our problem, not just her problem. I came up with an idea to help Princess get back on track in class, whether she was just clowning around, needed help with her work, or was seeking attention from either parent. It was important that I focus on putting her back on track. I called the school the next day and spoke with the principal about me visiting the school. We arranged for me to visit that Wednesday. I canceled every appointment I had scheduled that day. I might have lost a few dollars from work, but I was determined to give Princess the attention I received when my granny got phone calls from my school.

So I arrived at the school about nine o'clock, just after Princess. I walked into her class and when she saw me there in her school she was in total shock. I spent the entire morning and part of the afternoon in every class with her. At first I could tell she was a little embarrassed, but as time went on and her friends embraced me she relaxed. Not only did she enjoy my presence, but the other students enjoyed my being there as well. To be honest, I too enjoyed my stay. Her classes reminded me of things I had long forgotten. The students asked me for help with their projects, and the teachers were very thankful that I participated with the students. I even went out and bought pizza for the students for lunch. I can truly say it was a day well spent. It was dedicated to my daughter, but turned into an idea for me: teachers need more parents to participate in class. Not only does it help with the thirty-odd students they teach without an assistant; it also gives the parents an idea of what their children are learning. Since I visited the school I have received nothing but positive e-mails about Princess, and now she participates in class.

I also purchased a Bible* adapted for teenagers. It's the best book I could have bought for her as she comes into her teenage years. I got my Bible out and asked her to read hers to me. I showed her the book of Proverbs, one of the best books in the bible. It teaches children how to be obedient to their parents. It teaches them how to avoid becoming a part of a bad crowd. As we read the Bible she must have felt contrition in her heart. She went and brought a pillow she has had since she was a baby, opened up a secret compartment in it and gave me letters that had been sent from her school. She had taken them out of our mailbox. They dated back to November of 2009. The letters were about her disruptive behavior in class and the steps the teachers had to take. I decided then that we would read the Bible every night to help convince her of her wrongdoing. It also taught me a lesson: your child will try to outsmart you if you're not paying attention. The very next day I went and got myself a P.O. Box so that the mail from school no longer came to the house.

Now she's twelve years old and becoming a young lady, trying to learn her identity. I can certainly empathize: I've been there before.

CHAPTER FOUR

What I Have Learned

I am certain that as you read my life story many of you will find that you can relate to it. Some have more experiences than others in this lifetime; but it's up to each individual to not let the cycle continue to repeat itself. Oftentimes I have heard people say we are under a curse, or it's a generational curse. But if there is a generational curse, it is only because we don't initiate change in our lives. We continue the same pattern our parents and their parents followed. Exodus 19:5-6 reads,

> ***Thou shalt not bow down thyself to them, nor serve them: for I the Lord thy God I am a jealous God, visiting the iniquity of the fathers upon children unto the third and fourth generation of them that hate me; and shewing mercy unto thousands of them that love me, and keep my commandments.***

God has requested that we acknowledge and honor him first as the head and not the tail of our lives. God has simply expressed that he is a jealous God, and has left the decision in our hands whether or not to obey and respect his commandment. If we choose not to obey God, he punishes the children for the sins of the fathers to the third and fourth generation. Same goes for those who place other Gods before him—this means your job, your family, material things, and finances: whatever has taken your focus from God as the head of your life.

As parents, we don't want to deal with the fact that we've made bad choices ourselves, that we've taken wrong turns in life. We don't want to take responsibility for our own actions. This is why, I believe, we point fingers and blame everything and everyone else. We disregard the fact that we should teach ourselves to acknowledge God first before pursuing other things we want in life. Let us teach our children to acknowledge and respect God first, and then make everything else secondary. As parents, we must forgive what happened to us in the past. Our parents did what they were taught and what they believed was right for most of us. That was our parent's way of teaching as they learned through trial and error, or as their parents taught them. We can all look back and agree on one thing: in our parent's time of growing up their parents made sure the presence of God was in the home. There was respect inside as well as outside the home. It worked for them: it meant less killing, less stealing, and less disrespect for authority.

Now in today's generation the majority of our children don't have a clue what commandments God has given his people to follow. They have lost respect for their leaders. I hear the children address their parents by their first names, and the children answer their parents with these words: ***what, huh, yeah, nall.*** When I was growing up we said, "Yes, ma'am," or, "Yes, sir." We said, "Thank you," or, "No, thank you." One day when I was about ten years old I was outside playing with my friends, my granny called me and I answered her by saying "What?" Granny disappeared for about fifteen seconds, so I continued to play. By the time I turned around that stick she'd cut from the tree hit my legs. Granny's reply was, "I called you, now answer me again."

I immediately said "Ma'am." Point well taken. The word ***what*** never again came across my lips when I answeresd Granny or any other authority figure.

Nowadays little children sit with the adults as they talk in their homes. Conversations that are meant for adults' ears to hear should not be conducted in the presence of children. Little Susie can repeat word for word her parents' conversations or those of their adult friends. Let us start changing that with our children. Do not allow them to be in the midst of adults when adults gather to have conversations. Change the TV channels when they start to watch inappropriate TV shows. Do not allow them to hear or see things you don't approve of.

Most parents today have lost what it takes to keep the engine running in their children's everyday life. You might not be fortunate with money, but your teachings and words of leadership can stay forever throughout your children's lives. Remember Proverbs 18:21, which reads,

"Death and life are in the power of the tongue."

Speak the words and mean what you say to your children as well as to yourself. Your tongue is a powerful tool; your words hold weight and weigh heavy on your children's minds. Let us as parents take this a step further: when you speak positive things to the child, follow up with positive actions. Put their dreams on paper; keep it where it can be seen. At least three or four times a week speak of their dreams to them. Make it your business to become involved with your child's dreams. Your child might have dreams, but as they visualize their dreams, it will begin to manifest, and become reality. So if you speak positively, the reaction will be positive. If you speak negatively, your children's reaction will become negative.

One day I was sitting and talking with a friend of mine named Richard. I felt compelled to explain to him what I thought about his parenting skills. On several occasions I had heard him call his daughters bitches and hoes. Even in a normal conversation with his children, he would address his own daughters as bitches. I was in total shock the first time I heard this: he called them bitches as if he was saying to them, "I love you."

He explained to me that's just how he talks with his children, that he's teaching his children not to be soft. As I was on the outside looking in, regardless of how he was used to talking, I strongly felt it was totally disrespectful to his daughters. Those words should never have come out of his mouth to any human being, especially his daughters. I went on to say the young ladies you call ***bitches*** and ***hoes*** are your daughters, they should be treated like your princesses, regardless of what happened in the past with you. It is your duty to speak and release positive energy with your children.

Regardless of how bad Richard thinks his daughters are, or how angry he becomes, the word ***bitch*** should never leave his lips to express anger toward them. The power in the word ***bitch*** could create hatred toward him, the father, as well as in their entire outlook on life. His daughters to this day, resent him for the lack of respect they have received from him.

I explained this to him: it could really hurt their adult life. I told him that I strongly believed his daughters would take his behavior with them into their own personal relationships. In their dating lives his daughters would think being calling names like that would be okay. And why? Because they were used to hearing that type of language from their father, even though it wasn't right. In this particular situation the children's mom was deceased and their older sister was raising four siblings alone herself. The father, I felt, should have been more active as well. He felt the only thing the children needed was money, or the only time the children would call him was when they wanted money. As I began to speak with the children, I could see they definitely wanted more than their dad's money. They wanted his love and attention and the children would get his attention any way they knew how. If it meant acting out in school, selling drugs, or becoming pregnant, they were determined to gain their dad's love.

It surely weighed heavy on my mind, trying to understand the father's childhood. It was clear their father was dealing with problems from his own childhood that he had not dealt with himself. It's frightening to say that this world is filled with parents who have so many scars from their past; these interfere with their parenting skills for their own children. Mostly they excuse carrying their hurts into their parenting by saying, "It didn't kill me," or, "It happened to me." That's the point I want to address—yes, it did happen to many of you, and no, it did not kill you. But I can tell you this: it hurt you. Some parents today probably felt alone, worthless, or abandoned as children. Why would you as a parent now believe another human being would be able to be a success in life if that same behavior inflicted upon your life continued?

This is a perfect example why we need to become responsible for our own actions first. Then it will spill over to our children and they will grasp the concept of responsibility. If you were abused as a child or if you were made to fend for yourself, do me a favor—remember how you felt, and try to make a transition for your children. You understand it wasn't a pleasant feeling to you. So do something about your thinking process: for a change, start to seek help. This is affecting your children now. Make a change for your children so they don't feel alone, worthless, or abandoned in their lives.

It seemed like the more I would talk with Richard the more he felt like I was against him. The truth is he felt like I was against him probably because no one ever took the time to tell him: that is inappropriate language to use with any human being, especially your daughters. It was clear he needed an excuse to cover his behavior, instead of just admitting he knew his behavior was hurtful toward his children. I truly wanted to have him hear with someone else's ears, how he sounded when he disrespected his children. It is easy to tell someone to grow up, but it's up to that person not to feel self-pity or excuse bad behavior. He would say, "I am my father's child. I'm not nice."

I would reply to him, "Try to be more than nice. Your children need your guidance, loving care, and support. It's okay to be nice and leave the excuses at the door; it is your child's turn to feel love and warmth. Don't make the same choices your father made."

Some fathers believe the only way to teach their sons to survive is to show them how to be tough, teach them not to show signs of emotions. A lot of times when a young boy begins to cry, his father would tell him to suppress his cry: "Men don't cry." Clearly when the boy becomes a man he will carry what his father has taught him as a child. In many cases it hurts not to express your true feelings as a young boy, and it will show in adult life. Fathers, if you realize you have deep hurts as a result of the way your father spoke to you as a child, I suggest you go have a talk with your father. Release whatever hurt you have toward your father. A lot of times when men have a heart-to-heart talk with their fathers, it starts a healing process for them at that very moment. In many situations the father probably wanted to say to his son, "I'm sorry for how I treated you when you was growing up. I only treated you as my father treated me." At that time you should be able to release the anger you carried for years, and begin a new chapter in life in which you heal yourself. If you feel your parents or someone else you were close to disappointed you in the past, it's important that you release that anger in order to move into a positive direction with your children. Richard, I suggest you give yourself a fresh start and try to become the apple of your children's eyes. Discipline is one thing, but a harsh word to express your discipline will have a strong effect on your children for the rest of their lives.

"I feel before they look to some athlete, movie star, or rapper, we as parents should be the most effective image on our own children's lives."

Grandparents are deceased or put away in nursing homes; their children don't have time for them. Their children are too busy pursuing their own life dreams. Instead of the grandparents being involved, they have no clue what's going on with the seeds they have sown. It takes a village to raise a child. This means all the people who live in the household and around you. Today we call it our community. Parents, they're all our children; let that grandparent or great grandparent, neighbor, friend, Sunday school teacher, classroom teacher, and whosoever has good intentions participate in your children's upbringing. They have wisdom and your children need to know the struggle through which they came. Most of our youth have no clue as to where they come from. They couldn't even tell you the first thing about their family tree. Their focus has gone in the wrong direction. They have placed value on material things and substituted reality. We have allowed our children to not pay respect to those that have ruled over them. Our children have lost the respect for elders that we had in our time. If we keep our grandparents in place to give structure, and to tell the stories of where they come from, I guarantee the youth will develop a consciousness of what the struggle really meant. The youth of today have no clue; they've developed a don't-give-a-damn attitude. The village and we parents must change the way our children think and how they respond to society in today's world.

Ask yourself and answer each question:

Who is your child's role model? Your answer should be you, first, as the parents. I feel before they look to some athlete, movie star, or rapper, we as parents should be the most effective image on our own children's lives. Why? Because charity begins at home, before any place else. This is my seed that I brought into this world and it is my duty to teach him or her the values and principles of life.

What ground rules have you put together in your household for your children? We as parents need to assist children with developmental skills. Read to your children as much as possible. Speak with authority in your household. Help the child to understand as they develop who is in control. Never let your children control the situation; you as the parent should always feel in control. As your child comes into teenage years they want to venture down new avenues. It's important that we allow them to develop, but keep in mind, your guidance is important. Teenagers start to feel like it's their time to control their lives. They will test you as parents to see how willing you are to allow them to do as they please. Many teenagers develop strong opinions about what they want to do once they feel like they have the right to make their own decisions. It is okay for them to develop a strong personality, so long as it is with this clear thought in the back of their minds: "My parents must approve of all the decisions I make as a teenager." That's why I believe if you make your request known very clearly and early in the child's life, they might stray a little from what you have taught them, but not as much as if you don't take control at that early stage. They will respect your request if you enforce your daily requirements on them.

How often do you take the time to just listen to your child? I'm guilty of this too; hardly ever do I just listen. I have comment after every statement. Which makes the child think, "What's the point if I can't express my feelings??? There is no point in talking!" Sometimes our actions and words send them looking for answers in the wrong place. That's how they become associated with the wrong crowd. Your child's freedom of (respectful) speech has in a way been silenced by you, the parent. Children are human beings too, just trying to develop and come into their own identity. We must give them structure, but also be their listener. This world is not the same as it was twenty years ago. We as the parents can't say, "Do as I tell you to do, not as I do." We have all heard that saying, but the facts still remains—setting an example is critical for our children.

CHAPTER FIVE

Giving Your Child Guidance and Structure

From the moment your baby is born, the only way you can understand its needs is by paying attention to it. When a baby is hungry it gives a sign by smacking its lips together, or sucking on its fingers. When a baby has dirtied its diaper it will begin to move around to indicate, "Change my pamper." When a baby feels happy it gives you a smile. When a baby feels uncomfortable, whether from teething, a stomachache, or colic, they will begin to cry. During that time you will talk with the baby, and the baby will start to mimic what it has heard and seen as its mind develops each day. Soon, you have a toddler who's communicating through words and learning to walk, and whom you're assuring the next step is possible. But remember: children learn their language by repeating what you and others constantly say around them.

Some parents read to their children often; other parents hardly ever. This stage is challenging not only for the baby but for you as well. This is where you praise them for doing good acts, and you tell them no when they are doing wrong. The child that you nourished through the early stages of life now becomes able to follow and respect everyday life. During that period of your child's development it is very critical to participate in his or her life. Don't you agree? Yes, I strongly agree: that period is when morals and values are set in place.

Children must have guidance and structure early in life. It is a must that you give your child guidance (meaning leadership or direction). The parents are the leaders in the household. The children will look up to you as their parents for leadership, especially to the father. Fathers, whether you are in or out of the household, it is your duty according to the Bible:

> ***"Honor thy father and mother; which is the first commandment with promise."*** (Ephesians 6:2).

Also, remember Ephesians 6:4, which reads,

> ***"And, ye fathers, provoke not your childre to wrath: but bring them up in the nurture [meaning to give tender care and protection to a young child] and admonition [meaning advice for or against doing something] of the Lord."***

All parents have the responsibility to make sure they teach their children positive discipline and give them guidance. It is important to give them positive guidance because it promotes the development of positive self-control. The more time we as parents spend focusing on our children's positive behavior, the less time there is to focus on their bad behavior.

Parents, even when you place your child in a daycare program, or if a caregiver comes to your home, make sure you screen whoever will be in charge of your child. Make sure he or she promotes the same values and behavior. Do not allow anyone that participates in your child's life to give mixed signals to your child: when it comes to the guidelines by which you want your child to abide, have them set in stone. If you have more than one child in your home, remember to focus on each child individually; your children's behavioral problems most likely will not be identical. How you discipline one child might not work for the other children in your home. Each child has his or her own personality, so please keep that in mind. When your child demonstrates positive behavior, make sure you acknowledge them with praise, and remember to focus more on the positive behavior. A kind word will stimulate a positive reaction from your child. You could say, "Thank you for behaving so nicely," or, "I am proud of your behavior." Something that will promote them to continue positive behavior. Remember to key in on positive behavior with your child, focus more on what should be done rather than what shouldn't.

Often you will hear there isn't a manual or a script for parenting. I believe that's a poor excuse and parents need someone or something to blame for not taking responsibility for their own children. It is our responsibility not to bring our children to great anger, vengeance, or sin. We as fathers and mothers are to teach them how to love, and we can do this by giving them love. Let them know that when they become angry it's okay to show emotions, but also explain how to deal with anger. Do not allow your child to develop a negative attitude, or develop one yourself. Remember that your focus is on dealing with anger in a positive way. If you turn around and lash out at the child for misbehavior, you are promoting negative behavior patterns. With your teenage children, teach them what your values are in the home. Regardless of what they see in the outside world, it is all about what you continue to teach inside your home. We want our teenagers to understand that no good deed goes unnoticed; do unto others as you want others to do unto you. Pay attention to how they interact with others around them. Do they have a don't-give-a-damn attitude? Or are they concerned about others? Will they take responsibly of cleaning their rooms or taking out the garbage without you asking them to? It is time we stop pampering our teenagers: allow them to take responsibility for their own actions. Parents, how will they ever come to grips with the reality of the real world, if we as parents continue to do everything for them?

"Once you let up on your guidance strategy, that's when the rope that you have released gets tangled up."

Don't stop disciplining your children just because they reach a certain age. Once you let up on your guidance strategy, that's when the rope that you have released gets tangled up. The friends your teenage children hang out with—screen them to make sure they have similar guidelines in their homes.

That's when the comparisons begin between how you want your children to behave and how their friends' parents expect their children to behave. We as parents must stay close to our children, keep our ground rules in place, continue to give unconditional love, and our children won't stray too far from our teachings.

It is also important you continue to focus on positive behavior—what you will accept from your child. That way, when it comes to what you won't accept, it won't become such a big issue or concern for the teenager. During teenage years things become cloudy and confusing for teens. One minute they become so grown, they think they know it all, and they feel they can make their own decisions without their parents' input. Then the next minute a teen will become that dependent child again, wanting and needing parental input or advice. But the key words for the parent to remember will be: they are growing teenagers trying to find their identity and purpose in life. So parents, continue to stay visible at all times as your teenager is going through this phase. Whatever mind set your teen is in at that moment and time, you just remember to continue to oversee your teenagers' decisions in this stage of their lives.

As I mentioned before, your children are the product of what you demonstrate to them, as well as what you teach them. To the married couples: Mom, I hope you have chosen a man that meets your children's needs, as well as your own wants and needs. It is the father's responsibility to set ground rules and boundaries in the household. It is the mother's responsibility to echo what guidance and structure the father has put in place. Remember, Mom, you are the father's help partner. You are the cheerleader in essence. Do not allow that child to manipulate the plan the father has set in place for your household. Work with the father so that he can do his job as the head of the household.

If you're a single parent, ask yourself how often you involve your children in your dating life, and more importantly, how will you involve them?.

What standards, what qualifications are you looking for in your new partner? The most important thing should be how well that partner interacts with your children once he or she has been given the opportunity to become involved in your children's lives. What morals and standards can he or she bring into your environment? Ask yourself, will this be a good decision for us as a family? Don't get bit by the bug: you'd be surprised how many people look for a partner just to take care of them. But that will become more of a burden then a help to you. You really have to be at peace with yourself to find a partner that will fit your profile. If you rush into a relationship because you're just desperate or tired of being alone you might run into a brick wall. Because once you have let your emotions overtake your standards, and once you forget to go through the screening process, then you have extra nonsense on your plate. Nonsense that could have been avoided if only you had a strategic plan for your family. Remember, you are bringing up young ladies and gentlemen; it's important that you do not think selfishly during your dating process. Your children are watching and listening. Most of our children slip from under our noses when our attention is focused on other things. So be alert, take your time, and consider the children.

What has happened to the homes the children of this generation are growing up in? In many cases parents are overlooking the problem. How can we as parents be afraid to discipline someone we brought into this world? A lot of parents have become afraid because we allowed a situation with the child to get out of control. We as parents did not think it was necessary when little Johnny or little Susie was growing up to say no to them, or show them how you expect them to behave. So if they can get away without consequences with you the parent, they feel they can do it to other people who have authority over them. Some parents condone what their children do. They speak with them as if they were adults. Bad mistake: it gives children the impression that they can act out, as they consider themselves equal to the adult. A wake up call is what you need to give your children, let them know who is in control. Parents, it is now time to own up to what's happening with our children today. Day by day start to make it a habit to be more mindful when the children are present. We as parents will face trial and error, but it is up to us to make corrections when we see things are starting to go wrong.

Single parents, unfortunately, have to work twice as hard to put this guidance in place for our children. I know sometimes you feel alone, tired, and you might even feel defeated. Understand, though, this is the journey we have chosen to take. Nothing is promised to us but life and death.

Here are some key points that I think will give your assistance with your children. Make sure you maintain a particular standard in the home. Don't allow the child to persuade you to bend the rules you have set in place. Get control of the situation before it becomes a problem you cannot handle. Don't overlook a problem thinking it will rectify itself; remember, the more you overlook a problem, the bigger it gets. Provide a good example for your child, not just now and then: do it all the time. Praise your child for doing the right thing when he or she does it without your assistance, and without you having to request it. Encourage positive activities, and support the activities your child chooses to participate in. Parents, you cannot become tired of promoting guidelines. Don't become too comfortable, thinking your children will not do certain things. Don't take it for granted that your children will carry out what you taught them last week or last year. It must be presented to them on an everyday basis. Let your child's mind develop toward being obedient, committed, reliable, and passionate for themselves, other people, and other things.

When you decide to marry, this decision should be something you have thought about long and hard. I know getting married is a step we all wish to make one day. But as they say, "Rome was not built in one day." Marriage is the joining of one distinctive individual to another distinctive individual. Take your time, do your homework, know the individual you say you want to spend the rest of your life with. This is a covenant, meaning a mutual promise before God, which you are about to enter into. I speak from my own testimony: know the person to whom you about to say, "I do." Take as long as you need to get to know that unique individual. Ask all the questions you feel you should ask: if he or she truly wants to marry you, nothing should be left untold. Each individual should be willing to tell all about who they are. Never assume you know everything about a person if you have never asked. Never feel you have to be married just because someone finally asked the big question, "Will you marry me?" We often get excited about that question, due to feeling it might never be asked of us again. Truth be told, many people become excited more for the celebration than the actual commitment. Just remember your standards, what you will look for in the marriage, as well as what you will bring to the marriage. Remember also to visualize this individual parenting your children. A marriage is hard work and both unique individuals have to be willing participants in order to trust, love, and dedicate themselves to a covenant lasts forever.

Also, if you're a divorced parent and you've started to date other people, make sure your new partner accepts your children. Your new partner, I believe, should understand this was all here before he or she came into the equation. Make sure your new partner understands and is ready to accept the challenge of dealing with your past.

There should be a respectful boundary between the ex-spouses for the sake of the children. So I say to the single parents with that boy or girl, when you decide to become involved with a new partner, make sure you are looking for someone who completes your children as well as yourself. Make sure that their guidance and structure is what you believe in as well. Do not accept a partner just to remedy your loneliness, or just because you want to say you have a partner. It's important that your partner sees how you care for your children. Then you will be able to tell if your new partner approves of your guidelines, or if he or she even cares what you do with your children. Oftentimes when we find a partner we are not conscious of the fact that the partner will be around our children. It is usually more about curing our loneliness.

"You must keep in your mind at all times; your children are watching and paying close attention to your lifestyle."

If your partner also has children from a previous relationship, you should watch how that partner is with them. Is your partner actively involved with them, paying attention to their schooling and activities, celebrating their good behavior, and disciplining their bad behavior? How active your partner is with his or her own children is one of the key points you look for in your new relationship. If your new partner has a don't-give-a-damn attitude about parenting, you should be forewarned that he or she will have a similar attitude in your home around your children. Lights should start to flash: ***move on***. This is not the relationship you want to enter, not only for your sake, but for the sake of your children as well. We are on the path of teaching our children to become great leaders in their lives, and we want children who will one day take responsibility for their own actions. There is no time to waste teaching a new partner how you and your children deserve to be treated. If the new partner is not ready, I strongly suggest you become unavailable and move on. Make room in your life for the man or woman who is ready. I have often heard the saying, "Let go, and let God deal with whatever you are going through." You must keep in your mind at all times; your children are watching and paying close attention to your lifestyle.

They will hold you accountable for your leadership and direction. That is what has been written; let it become your daily manual.

Single parents, pray or do whatever you believe in, so that you keep a calm, healthy atmosphere in your home. Do not think you have to make a relationship happen—it will happen when you least expect it to happen. It is not your responsibility to teach a partner how to love you: he or she should already be willing and ready to demonstrate love, guidance, and structure that fit you and your children like a glove. You do not want hateful, selfish, vindictive, murderous, robbing, stealing, spirits to surround you, your children, or your home. Keep all negative spirits away from you and your children. Your children will demonstrate whatever behavior pattern they see inside the home. If your new partner takes responsibility for the upkeep of your home, then that will be a positive image for your children to see, and they will feel like they should take care of the home as well. If your new partner sits around and watches you take care of the home, then your children will think, "Why should I do anything?" If your new partner respects the household and comes home at a respectable time, then the children will respect what time they come home. If your new partner hangs out at all times of the night, then your teenage children will think it okay to hang out all night. This will send mixed messages to the children, especially if they have not seen this type of behavior before your new partner entered your home. Stay on the right path of leadership, structure, and guidance in your home, and your everyday life.

Ex-spouses, I know you have pillow talk with your new partner about issues that might arise with your ex-spouse, but it's important that your new partner never step to your ex-spouse as if he or she has a right to address the ex-spouse about your children or a previous situation of which he or she has no knowledge. Especially if this is all new to all parties involved. It is best for your new partner to stay neutral in you and your ex-spouse's affairs. Work out the problems between the two of you, so that bitter feelings don't enter. It's okay for your new partner to address you during your pillow talk, if they're giving you good advice about handling situations with the children. But that is as far as it should go. Don't allow the boundaries to be crossed.

Also, when the children visit the ex-spouse, the ex-spouse should have a talk with them about any new partner he or she is dating, especially if the new partner lives with your ex-spouse. It is important that children respect the new partner, and that the new partner respects the children. Never allow the new partner to show jealousy toward your children when they are with you. Some new partners tend to forget that your attention will be focused on the children while they visit. Although that can feel flattering and appear attractive in your new partner, soon it becomes a problem and is not so attractive. Take your children one-on-one and spend time with them away from your new partner. It is important just to have a talk about how your child is coping with the situation. It's good to listen and get feedback from your children and to reassure them you will always be there as their parent. ***The children need to have that one-on-one time with you.*** Learn what your children are thinking; ask them how they feel about the new situation. You never know: the new partner might be mistreating your child while you are away at work. If your child is being mistreated you want to stay informed. It must be prevented. The child might feel rebellious against your new partner, just because your new partner is not the child's parent. Try to keep things safe and fair for all parties. I know it's work, but the children are what matter and the safety of the child is more important than anything else. Once each party becomes very familiar and feels comfortable, then start to introduce other things gradually.

Divorced or separated parents should handle disagreements between their children and their new partners. Don't let problems escalate: take charge of both parties and mediate between them. Sometimes the new partner feels like he or she has something to prove. If so, keep a close watch, because the only thing the new partner should feel is, "I'm here to make it better and as smooth as possible; I know it's a transition for the children." It's your responsibility to your child to know when your child is having a real problem with your new partner and when your child only wants your attention. Either way, find the root of the problem. Then you and your ex-spouse can put it in perspective. This will help create a more peaceful home while your children are in your care.

CHAPTER SIX

Some Food for Thought

Structure means organization, arranging something into a whole: Please place your toys back in the toy box when you're finished playing with them. Please make your bed and clean your room. Please be in the house by 9:00 p.m., your curfew time. That's what you call organization of their minds. You have to first show them by example, and then you must continue to speak of that example to the child. Then it will become a normal routine in your child's everyday life. Once you let up on how you want things to be organized in your home, your child will begin to think a given chore doesn't have to be done today, or the next day, and so on. But if you lead by example and speak the words by which you want them to abide in your home, it will automatically become part of your life and your child's everyday life too. The child will become accustomed to giving you what you expect. We as parents tend to slack up on our children. We become too busy with our own lives. Maybe it's because you work longer hours, maybe it's because you've enrolled in school and wish to complete your education, or maybe it's because you need some time alone. Whatever the case may be, don't forget to have the key elements in place for your children while you pursue the other goals of your life. There should always be a balance between your family, your career, and your social life.

CHAPTER SEVEN

School

One day, when I was talking to Princess's doctor, he asked me why Princess had come to him during school hours. I explained she was in discomfort from a rash she had developed. He replied that could have waited until the end of the school day. It is important she receives her education first, the doctor said to me.

I replied, "I am the parent and she had only a half-day in school today."

The doctor went on to explain why he even bothered to tell me anything about which priorities should be placed first. Dr. Cho said when he came to America he was in the sixth grade. When the American school system tested him for placement he tested at the ninth grade level in every subject. That encouraged me to go and do my homework about our educational programs, and the curriculum being offered in American public schools. Dr. Cho asked: "Are American children really being prepared for college? Or will they be playing catch-up when it is time to enter college?"

I also looked at education systems in other cultures, such as Japan, only to discover that their public grade schools are way more advanced than our American schools. One writer describes Japanese schools in detail:

> Japanese school buildings are plain, but functional. Generally, they are three-story, rectangular, concrete structures which lack central heating or air conditioning... The lack of decoration and furnishings is believed to help the child focus on learning and building character. Yet all schools have excellent educational facilities, including libraries, music rooms, art rooms, gymnasia,

and playgrounds. Seventy-five percent of public schools have swimming pools. Music rooms ordinarily include electric organs, pianos, xylophones, percussion instruments of various kinds, and often a ruled blackboard suitable for teaching music reading. Science and art rooms are similarly well equipped.

Teachers teach a different grade level each year, thus gaining broad experience with the curriculum and characteristics of all six grades… Talented and experienced teachers are more frequently assigned to the 1st grade because that stage is considered critical in establishing children's attitudes and learning habits for the rest of their school lives.

[In math] children in Japan are introduced to many concepts such as decimals, fractions, and geometric figures earlier than their American counterparts. Accuracy in computation is stressed more than the ability to estimate. More emphasis is placed on geometry, ratios, proportions, and reading charts than in most American elementary schools.

In the 5th and 6th grades, Japanese boys and girls receive two hours of instruction per week in basic homemaking skills. The goal is to deepen children's appreciation of and participation in family life. Children practice basic meal planning and learn how to prepare and serve simple foods. They learn to take care of their own clothing, including hand washing of various articles, sewing buttons, and mending seams. They also practice making simple articles like bags and aprons and decorating them with simple embroidery.

> Although occupying only one class hour per week, moral education has a fundamental role in Japanese education. It is a distinct area of instruction at every level of compulsory education, and attitudes, habits, and behaviors which are consistent with the Japanese value system are infused throughout the curriculum.
>
> The Japanese concept of moral education is far from vague or formless. Twenty-eight themes in six categories are covered at the elementary level. [2]

In physical education Japan values sports, exercise, and the development of strength and perseverance. Their children are also taught about "achieving and maintaining good health," which means less obesity in their children. They are also taught about nutrition and traffic safety. Taught to swim by the time they are in sixth grade, their children are competent and confident in the water.

The Japanese attend school six days a week; yes parents, that means Saturday from nine to noon.

Parents everywhere: we need to start helping our children receive a better education. They need to learn moral education in school, take swimming classes in grade school, and learn about nutrition and how to prepare a meal before entering high school. Most importantly: advance our math curriculum. Here in Chicago we have a great educator by the name of Marva Collins, who famously said, "Don't try to fix the students, fix ourselves first. The good teacher makes the poor student good and the good student superior. When our students fail, we, as teachers, too, have failed."

Parents, our children's education should be our primary interest starting with the first day they are introduced to school. Our public schools here in the United States only give a basic introduction to education. They must do more, especially in the first through fifth grades, as this is when our children establish the attitudes and learning habits that will define who they are for the rest of their student lives. It is time we as parents really get involved in what our children's curriculum and activities are while in school. When it is time for our children to be introduced to grade school, it's important we the parents and the school staff enforce well-organized personal habits: how to sit in class, how to arrange the desktop for study, polite use of language, and proper behavior and classroom routines.

As our children continue their education in grade school, we must ask ourselves, what is being taught in social studies, math, science, music, arts and crafts, and physical education? Are they truly being prepared to go on to the next level of education, i.e., high school and college? These are questions we as parents should ask as we become more involved with the schools and make sure our children are prepared for the next level of education.

Get familiar with your child's teachers. Do you know your cell phone could keep you in communication with every one of your child's teachers? Well it can, in the same way you access Facebook, Twitter, MySpace, YouTube and other websites on it. Teachers now have e-mail addresses that they would gladly provide you with, just to inform you of your child's progress and participation each day in their classroom.

During your child's grade school years, how much of social studies time is devoted to the child's own school, family, and the communities they reside in? When does the emphasis expand to the city, the nation, foreign countries, and learning to understand maps, graphs, tables, and world geography? When your child enters that math class, the basics of math should be introduced: addition, subtraction, multiplication, and division. In the science classroom our children develop the ability to observe and to conduct simple experiments about the life of plants, animals, and humans. Our children learn about matter and energy, and also the earth and the universe are studied through the weather and atmospheric phenomena, geology, and erosion. It is a plus to have music in the classrooms: it gives the child pleasure to be able to hear different types of music, and also to learn different languages in music.

Make sure we participate in their interests in school. Ask them what happened in school each day. Learn the struggles they have to face there, and help them to overcome their struggles. Don't let them feel defeated about the problems they are having in school. Physical education in our schools begins with the enjoyment of games, sports, also through physical exercise and physical health practices. Visit and participate with your child at school to see what other programs and studies are involved with your child's everyday learning.

Encourage your children to participate in every class they attend. Let them know it's okay not to understand every assignment that the teacher hands out. But make sure that if they don't understand something they ask the teacher for help. Also, encourage your children to surround themselves with positive children in the classroom. Back when I attended grade school, teachers communicated with parents through a telephone call, or a note that had to be returned with a parent's signature. If that note came home to our parents back then, and it was a bad report about our behavior, we knew repercussions followed. Also, by the time you arrived at school the next day, you would be shocked to find your parent already there in school having a meeting with your teacher: no appointment was needed for parents to visit the teachers. That would be so embarrassing because not only did you feel like you were in trouble; the ***oohs*** and ***aahs*** of the kids in your classroom confirmed that you were in trouble. But that one visit was all it took for most of us to get our act together. Teachers had concern for the children back in the day. Teachers rarely felt threatened by students or even parents. Teachers felt like parents were on board with their children's education. They also felt it was okay to give a student punishment as well. "Go stand in the corner; place your face against the wall. Write 100 times, ***I will not talk in class.***"

If your name went on the board, that meant no recess or gym for you that day. You would also be made to move your desk right next to theirs for the rest of the day.

I attended John P. Altgeld School on the south side of Chicago. I had a teacher named Mrs. Murray in the fifth grade. To this day I can hear her calling my name: "Jonetta, quiet in my class." If I wouldn't stop talking I knew a phone call would be placed to Granny or Mom. Today I thank Mrs. Murray and remember how she took time out with each of her students on a daily basis.

From the principal on down to the teachers, all knew my granny very well. They weren't afraid to pick up the phone and call the parents back then. The parents and teachers were all in accord. They were willing to raise the child together. If the child got out of control and needed to be disciplined, the teachers and the parents disciplined the student. It was a relief to the parents to know that the teachers took the time to show concern for the child. Nowadays the teachers are afraid to say anything to the child. Most of the teachers feel threatened by the students. Some parents don't want the teachers to look at the child in a mean way, not to mention discipline them.

Schools are not as inviting as they were back in the 1980s and 1990s. Now when you enter most of our schools you have to be strip-searched like you are going into a courthouse. Metal detectors and officers greet you now when you enter public schools. The students are killing, selling drugs, and fighting right in the schools. It's a scary sight to enter some of our public schools. This all starts because these children have lack of respect for authority, especially their parents.

Key points for communicating with teachers: check your child's timetable book daily and request that they give you a daily report when coming home from school; if you are at work, place a phone call home to ask how your child's day went at school; if your child receives a note home from school, take time to go visit with that teacher. Make sure all your contact information is correct so that the school can reach you.

As I stated before, your cell phone is a great tool for communicating with the teachers. Just as you receive e-mail on your computer, you can receive e-mails on your cell phone. A lot of parents have Facebook, Twitter, and MySpace on their cell phones and faithfully check them daily, sometimes two to four times a day. Well, check your e-mails daily for your child's progress in school.

Get into your child's business; first of all, they have no business without your approval. Most importantly, set a goal at the beginning of the school year for your child. Stick to the plan and when you see your child slacking, or if your child needs help, go the extra mile and help. We as parents want our children to be successful in their endeavors. Post a list of their goals in a place where it can always be seen. That will keep them on task for the next assignment. Also, a lot of parents tend to want their children to become what they wanted to become in life. It's okay to have dreams for your child, but let them make the choice of what they want to become. Do not force your dreams onto your child. Whatever they are interested in becoming let them become.

CHAPTER EIGHT

Minding Your Child's Business

As parents we forget what we are supposed to be focused on. It's not that we don't care about our children; sometimes we just take it for granted they will do what we expect them to do. For the most part, children will continue to follow the right path after we express what behavior we will accept. But we should not become too comfortable. Check on your child as often as you think you should. We as parents become so involved in what is going on in our everyday personal life that we forget what's going on in our homes. It's not done intentionally: many of us parents deal with a lot of pressure from the outside world, and when we finally come home we just take it for granted that our household is in order. Our children get accustomed to our day-to-day routines and begin to think they can outsmart us. We have to dedicate just as much attention and time to our children as we dedicate to our outside responsibilities. Start to change your pattern in your home. Ask your child to check in with you every hour, so that you can be aware of what your child is doing, and most importantly where your child is going.

When you come home from work, don't just ask your child, "Did you do your homework?" Ask to see it. Your child should never feel they don't have to disclose to you as the parent what they have done in your absence, where they went, and whom they were with. It's your right as a parent to know all of the above, and it is your right to mind their business. If we followed the way most of what our parents taught us, the child would think twice before they made decisions without consulting with you as the parent first. Remember the saying: "If it's not broke, don't fix it."

I'm not talking about being abusive—only about being aware of who your child is. Reading their diaries and journals would give you a great idea of your child's state of mind. We as parents should know what our children feel within themselves. You will find out if the child is happy or sad. You'll find out whether the child has been sexually active or abused, has been using or selling drugs, thinking of bombing a school, or if your child has built up hatred for an individual. Sometimes parents just can't see a problem accruing with their child: either they're out trying to provide for their child, or they're just totally detached from their responsibilities as parents. So it's important to do a routine check on your child. Clean their rooms more often. Some children are on the right path, but then some are not on the right path. Children look at their rooms as their comfort zones and feel that's where everything they have can be placed or even hidden. Many of our children go straight to their rooms when they come home from school. Sometimes with the door shut to keep others from entering. They play their games in their rooms, watch TV in their rooms, and even have dinner in their rooms. That's entirely too much time spent alone in their rooms. Get to know what drives them straight to their rooms.

A lot of our children also have their own computer in their rooms. It's important we as parents pay attention to the websites our children enter. The Internet can be used as a good tool for our children when they have homework assignments. But keep in mind that your children can surf the Internet for anything you could imagine, or should I say can't imagine. We as parents need to stay just a notch above our children to protect them from what's on the Internet. Check your children's computers to see if they're joining inappropriate chat rooms or reading blogs that don't promote positive knowledge. Our children can learn how to make bombs or meet people who pretend to be someone they really aren't. Put on the parental control when you allow your children to be on the Internet: online safety is the key.

Teen sexuality is an important subject you and your child should definitely talk about before he or she becomes sexually active. I know we, as parents would like for our teenagers not to have sex, to wait until they are married. But in reality, if we as parents don't discuss sex with them, someone else will. It's a subject that should not be taken lightly. When you feel the time is appropriate to discuss sex and sexuality with your teenagers, don't hesitate: educate your teenager about sex. It's important we as parents teach how to prevent unwanted pregnancy and sexually transmitted disease. Talking about sex with your teenager might seem uncomfortable at first, but the more you talk about it the more comfortable it gets. Talking about sex should not be a one-time conversation; it should be repeated so long as you feel the need to continue to educate the teen. We want to build a trusting relationship with our teens.

When talking about sex, make sure you ***listen*** to your teenagers. It might not be something we as parents want to hear from our children, but just listen: don't become upset. Take a deep breath: don't punish or judge your son when he reveals to you what's on his mind or what he's already done. Remember to talk about your values and morals. Your main goal is to teach how to prevent unwanted situations. Whether you daughter is sexually active or not, keep it in her mind how to protect herself from diseases and emotional damage. You want to stress the topic of birth control, its different forms (pill, condoms, and so on), where it can be obtained, and how to use it as well. Talk about not being pressured into having sex with anyone: it's okay to say no. Let your child know, no matter what choice they make you are there for them, and will educate them.

When dealing with STDs, gather all the information that you can. You'll want to talk about chlamydia, genital herpes, gonorrhea, syphilis, venereal warts, and HIV/AIDS. Educate yourself about HIV/AIDS: it is fatal, has no cure, and is considered an epidemic in the African American community. So, parents, it might be uncomfortable to talk about sexuality, but guess what? It will save your child's life.

Also, unwanted pregnancy is so common today. When I was growing up, if a girl became pregnant it was a shock not only in the household, but also on the block and in the community. It was not seen as a fad or looked at as "just another" young pregnancy. It was something that was kept a secret from others until you actually could see the girl's stomach growing bigger. The young girl would feel she had made a bad choice and would feel ashamed of what she had done. It was not looked on as a cause for celebration, but as a life change, a responsibility.

When I was about thirteen when the neighbor's daughter Randy became pregnant. She was about fifteen. Right when my granny learned Randy was pregnant I received my first speech. Granny wanted to plant the seed in my mind: if and when I felt the need to have sex, tell her or my mom first. She also stressed the fact that when she was young, if a girl became pregnant at a young age the adults would use the expression "the girl has broken her leg." Granny went on to say that it was okay if I spoke to Randy if the two of us were outside, but I could no longer be in her company. I said to my granny, "Isn't that a hurtful thing to say, since my friend has become pregnant I can no longer be in her company?

She replied by saying, "No, that is not a hurtful thing to say. I don't want you to be distracted from what's important and what you must be focused on in this stage of your life. Education is your focus and what you want to become in life should be your thought process at this age. Not a conversation about some young girl having to experience the pressure of becoming pregnant. In time, when you become married or of age to have a baby, that conversation will be appropriate."

As a young person I felt like I should be able to be friends with whomever I was pleased. I explained to my granny that I had good judgment and that I wouldn't become pregnant just because my friend had. Granny said, "That is good to hear you say, but what I have expressed to you is final, and you will obey just that."

It's extremely important that we mind our children's business. It will prevent a lot of unwanted situations in their lives. Your children might become rebellious if they think you're invading their privacy. Remember, you are doing what's best for them, and as they become older they will accept it, and respect that you acted for the sake of their well-being.

To our young teenage parents, it's a good idea to take some sort of parenting class to get an idea on what to expect of your little one, and who will be your support, that's extremely important. You have no clue when you become pregnant how much love and tender care your little one requires. Don't become overwhelmed, or so frustrated that you find yourself yelling, screaming, or shaking the baby, because you feel this task is too much for you to handle. When you get to that point, ask your support team—whether it's Mom or a close relative that you trust—to assist you with your little one. Remember, this is your pride and joy, God's gift, and it's given to you for you to love and keep away from all hurt, harm, and danger. As a young parent you have now taken the oath: ***My Child, My Responsibility***.

As a young person I felt like, "I should be able to do me," as the young people say today. But deep down inside, I'm grateful I had a mom and grandparents who cared enough to help steer me into doing what was best for me. Now that I am a parent, I find myself feeling the same way as my mom and grandparents felt: I'm a concerned parent. It's important I tell my children what is out in this world—good as well as evil.

This is a true story. My oldest son, Javonte, wanted to date a young girl who smoked pot. I thought to myself that if she smokes pot, let me check Javonte's room to see if he is also smoking pot. I decided to have a "mind my child's business day" in his room. That's what I call it in my home. So I proceeded to clean his room; I checked his drawers; I changed the linens on his bed; I checked his closet. I came up with nothing. As I was leaving his room a shoebox peeked at me from underneath his bed. Bingo, the shoebox had marijuana in it! Javonte thought he had hidden the pot in a place where I couldn't find it. Wrong, I told him. Been there, done that.

After finding the pot in my home I went off my rocket just a tad bit much. Here I was, yelling and screaming at the top of my lungs, about to send myself to the emergency room. Mr. Javonte was sitting on the bed giving me a look, as if he wanted to say, "This woman is going to need the paramedics sooner then she thinks."

In the midst of my performance a thought came to my mind: this yelling and screaming isn't fazing this child one bit. I left his room and went and sat at the kitchen table to collect my thoughts. At that time I was looking for a used car for him. So I told him, "You will not get a car until I am certain you are not using drugs." He needed to gain my trust again and to be more responsible. I stood my ground and wanted him to understand that the bad choices you make in life come with consequences.

I found myself taking on the same roll my granny would have taken with me. Granny would not leave anything untouched when she "cleaned my room." Every drawer, shoebox, or hiding place she thought I could have in my room she searched. Granny let it be known there would be nothing of mine in her house that she didn't buy for me. If it wasn't a gift from family or friends, she would ask who bought it, what did I do to receive a gift from that person? You better believe I had to answer her questions or that gift would be returned: it was just that simple. You see, Granny didn't fear her children; we knew what she would or wouldn't tolerate. Yes, I received whippings, but I didn't feel I was abused. When my grandfather spoke his words with authority, our household started to move around—very seldom did he resort to whippings. When he taught the family or one of us how to do something he would start by saying these words: "I will teach you this one time and one time only." That meant that wherever your mind or your attention was at that moment, it needed to focus on grandfather's voice. You also had to repeat back to him what he had just told you. My grandparents demonstrated how they were taught: spare the rod, spoil the child. On the other hand, they also demonstrated the love, values, and morals that their mothers and fathers taught them. It was clear to me that they gave us love. They gave us knowledge they themselves were taught.

I can't remember Granddad ever having a fight with Granny. Not in front of the children, not behind closed doors, not ever. But if they did, it wasn't a yelling match, or hands being thrown. It was them simply having a conversation and my grandfather coming out with the final say. Granny's opinion was taken into strong consideration and nine times out of ten it became a big part of my grandfather's solution to the problem. It was called respect for each other, as well as putting both heads together to work through the problem. That meant the potential for divorce was slim to none. Those marriage vows— until death do us apart—meant something. Whatever dirty laundry my grandparents had, the family never knew about it until both of them had died. Then it became only speculation or hearsay, what our grandparents went through.

In today's households those family values are very rare. Most married couples today, argue and fight right in front of the children. Nothing in the home is kept away from the children. But whatever you're going through in your marriage, it should really be kept between you and your spouse. Arguments should never get to the point where the children feel unsafe. What are we as parents teaching the child? How can you be dedicated to your family when your mind is not at ease? My answer is, we can't be dedicated to them, or teach them how to be calm or dedicated to anything. We are teaching our children to fight through problems instead of work through them. So

I suggest that before you start to mind your child's business you take time to bring yourself to a level of calmness. Get your thoughts together first. Parents, remember this is about the comfort of our children. Their minds are wondering, looking for leadership and answers. I believe we owe our children some tranquility, freedom from war in their own households. Parents, pull it together when you disagree, especially in front of your children.

Parents, let us also admit when we are wrong about something. Say to your child, "I was wrong." Take responsibility for your actions. Allow your child to see that when you have said or done something wrong you are capable of admitting it. I know it's hard to say those words. Take a deep breath and release: "I was wrong." It will teach them to admit openly when they have done something wrong. I know you are the parent; it's a learning experience with your children. Don't get caught up in always being right. That's not the real world: we as parents have made mistakes too. It's now time that we correct our mistakes, and let our children see that parents are human beings as well. It will teach them to think, "Okay, I made a mistake. Now how do I correct it?"

CHAPTER NINE

Child Abuse

Parents, as I address each of these topics, I pray all is fair and well with your children. Take time and learn to identify signs of an abused child: whether the abuse is mental, physical, or sexual. When a child is abused, most times the offender is someone close: our partner, family members, friends, or even ourselves. The abuse sometimes is right under our nose. If you feel your child has been abused in any way, take time to observe the situation. If your child flinches at your every move, seems withdrawn, scared, or fearful about doing something wrong, that's an indication something is wrong. Especially if the child isn't acting normally. If your child doesn't seem attached to either parent, or to any relative or friend, that could be a sign of child abuse. If you, your partner, a family member, or a friend was abused in childhood, you should know firsthand of that experience. Remember how you felt when someone mentally, physically, or sexually assaulted you. Whatever abuse you have experienced as a child, you don't want your child to go through this horribel experience as you did. When you are abused you begin to isolate yourself from others. Abuse changes the personality of an individual. Abuse is a horrible thing to experience, since one feels alone under the circumstances. Confusion runs through the victim's mind. Why me? We ask. What did I do to deserve this type of treatment from someone I thought I could trust? Should I tell someone about what just happened to me? Will the person I choose to confide my nightmare to, believe me? All types of questions enter the mind when someone is abused. It is important to explain to our children before they become victims of abuse that you are there for them no matter what situation they find themselves in.

Even if abuse never attacks your child, let them know how you feel about it, and what the child should do if confronted with it. Talk about it—don't let it happen that your child has no understanding about what to do, whom to turn to, or what to say. Don't let the cycle of abuse continue; it breaks your personality down. You develop low self-esteem; in some cases you become violent in your adulthood. Oftentimes, if you were mentally or physically abused as a child, it may seem natural to become abusive to your own children. But the fact of the matter is, you were being abused. There is a big difference between being abusive and being a disciplinarian. When you are an abuser you treat that child cruelly. You inflict bodily harm on a regular or habitual basis. You tend to speak insultingly to your child on a regular or habitual basis. This really hurts your children: they start to withdraw from their surroundings. The children are left in a situation where they don't feel good about themselves, they start to demonstrate signs of depression, and they start to act like they're worthless. They speak low of themselves, as if they don't matter in this life.

Christy was my best friend throughout seventh and eighth grade, and she would often tell me she was depressed. Christy would walk around with her head down low; she would often say she was sad and unhappy. As I look back, I recall that Christy wasn't very active in class; she was withdrawn and rarely participated. She thought no one really liked her in school, and would always stay to herself. I think I was one of the few children she would interact with in school. Now, looking back, I really believe she was being either mentally or sexually abused. But I being a kid with a loving family, I was unable to see this at the time. I just felt Christy was a quiet individual who wanted to please her mom. I often asked her, "Why are you always depressed?" Her only answer was, "I feel like a failure." I couldn't understand that, because she had good grades in school. What else did she need to prove? She was a good kid,

I thought to myself. When we were children, I would say to her, the only thing that counts is that we get good grades, obey our parents, and live a carefree life. But she would say, "I'm depressed throughout the entire school year."

Years went by without me ever thinking my friend was a victim of abuse. Then, when I was about twenty-three years old, I bumped into her again. The first thing I asked her was, "How are you doing? Have you been okay?" She revealed to me that she was a victim of mental abuse as a child. Nothing she did or said was good enough for her mom. A light bulb came on in my head. I asked her, "Is that why you were always depressed in grade school?"

She replied, "Yes. To this day I'm still fighting with depression." I hugged her right away and told her I was sorry for what she went through. I told her to not let that hold her life back. "You are somebody, and you matter to yourself in this lifetime." We exchanged phone numbers, but I walked away from that conversation feeling like I should have paid more attention to my friend.

Just knowing my friend was abused gives me discomfort. It is not a good feeling to be abused. Parents, don't let the anger you have built up inside be taken out on your precious little ones. Sometimes our children can do some of the most outrageous things. Ask yourself, is this for attention or is it a cry for guidance? Whichever it might be, don't come to an immediate judgment. Don't call the child names, and don't do bodily harm to the child. Most importantly, you the parent should take time out; go to the closet, bathroom—wherever you need to go. Count to ten. Grasp what just happened with your child. It is sometimes better just to walk away from a heated situation and realize what just took place. Find a way to learn how to be calmer when dealing with your children in everyday life situations. It's important that you talk about your abuse; if you don't take the time to get help, your child is likely to become a victim of child abuse or child neglect.

Child obesity is another form of child abuse, and a result of child neglect. It is a strong topic in my home. It is a situation that Princess and I deal with every day. We as parents become comfortable with feeding our children foods we think are fast to prepare, or maybe we don't feel like cooking as much. But in reality we are teaching our children to eat unhealthy foods and drink unhealthy beverages. How often do we as parents pay attention to the food our children consume each and every day, or the calories they put into their bodies? Probably almost none of us pay attention.

I am very guilty of that: after my divorce I was in survival mode. I was more focused on how to provide a better life for my children financially, and I couldn't focus on what my children and I were putting in our bodies. When I shopped for groceries I would purchase a lot of unhealthy junk food: cookies, cakes, pies. Princess would come home from school, drop her book bag, and go straight for the fridge. Sometimes she would have a snack or a sandwich before she began her homework. Why? Because I had become so busy with my own life. I was caught up with just providing for the household. Many of us are single parents and have a lot going on in our lives: we're working long hours to make ends meet or going to school to further our education. In the process of trying to provide a better life for our children, we neglect to enforce good eating habits.

What causes our children to gain extra unwanted weight? I believe it's lack of exercise, stress in the household, peer pressure, depression, and most of all, poor eating habits. If we don't take care of these things, we all risk becoming unhealthy human beings. Did I think of the possibility that Princess might get high blood pressure, or that she might have thyroid problems, or other health issues? No, I did not. I just thought that one day she would grow out of being a little overweight. The habit of eating unhealthy foods is very hard to break. Children look at the healthy food as being a dreadful medicine they must eat. We as parents have to be firm and make the transition from unhealthy to healthy foods each and every day, and include exercise into our weekly agendas. Now that Princess has started to eat healthier, she wants to teach other youths how to exercise, and how to choose a piece of fruit before a candy bar.

CHAPTER TEN

Detecting Child Abuse

A young man named Thomas once confided to me that he was sexually assaulted as a young boy. Thomas's parents would take him to a day care provider every day of the week. When his parents dropped him off there, Thomas would cry, imploring his parents not to leave him. His parents never really paid attention to his cries; they thought it was just Thomas not being used to them leaving him. They felt they were leaving their son in good hands with the care provider: she attended the same church they did, and had been friends with the family for years. Living in her home with her, the day care provider had two sons older than Thomas and one son the same age. Thomas told me how one of the older sons, Frank, would touch Thomas's private parts. Thomas had always known Frank, so he trusted him. Frank wasn't a stranger to Thomas at all; Thomas would play with Frank's youngest brother, Robert, at church all the time. Frank persuaded Thomas to perform sexual acts with him. Thomas was very uncomfortable with Frank's behavior, but never said a word to his parents. Thomas felt like Frank was a true friend; he looked at Frank as an older brother, and as a protector. Thomas also told me he could remember his provider speaking with Frank about how he had grown attached to Thomas. How Frank would want Thomas to follow him wherever he would go. Frank had taken on a strange interest in Thomas; he would give Thomas things he liked to gain his trust more and more every day. Frank had no interest in the other children at the day care that Thomas was aware of.

Thomas believed, he told me, the daycare provider had reason to know about her son's behavior, but she didn't want to face reality of her son's attraction to the same sex. Thomas said she should have known about her son's feminine behavior, because he would take an interest in girl's activities—playing with dolls, and wearing her high heels—at fifteen years of age. The mother would never question Frank about his behavior; maybe she thought it was a phase and the problem would eventually correct itself.

Oftentimes, we as parents see negative behavior in our children, but say nothing about it. Either we're in denial, or we don't want to face the problem head on. Frank had both parents at home; both parents attended church as well. Clearly they swept their child's behavior under the rug by not addressing the problem. It allowed an innocent individual to become hurt sexually, mentally, and emotionally.

Thomas never told his parents of Frank's behavior. He completely blocked Frank's sexual behavior out of his mind. Or so he thought. Thomas was dealing with the mental and emotional impact of being sexually assaulted. As he grew older and started to date women, he never really understood why he would cheat on his girlfriends. Thomas could never be faithful to any of the young ladies he dated. For a long time he thought cheating was just part of being young. Thomas would tell himself that every young person cheats, but deep down inside he was carrying around the wound of how he had been sexually violated as a young boy.

Thomas went on to marry, still carrying around what had happened with him in his childhood. He was not faithful to his wife. When he lost her, he realized why he would cheat on every woman he had been with. He always kept in the back of his mind he had something to prove to himself: his masculinity. He took on this attitude: the only way to prove he was not a homosexual was to sleep with every woman he came in contact with. He was dealing with this low self-esteem, but at the same time took on this fake identity. He also carried the stigma of shame through the years. He blamed himself for Frank sexually assaulting him. Not until he confided to his parents the deep dark secret he had carried within him for years, and not until he received counseling from his minister, did he realize it was not his fault. He realized that being molested hurt his confidence, his self-esteem, his personality, and most importantly, it affected his ability to trust other people.

Frank's behavior could have been prevented. We as parents see signs of things and never question them. Frank is currently serving a life sentence for murder without the possibility of parole. I know Frank's parents look back and say we saw the signs but chose to ignore them. We overlook things our children do sometimes; we assume they know what's right and what's wrong. But how should they know what's right or wrong, if we as parents overlook the signs given to us?

Ask your children if anyone has ever touched them. Do not disregard the fact that you might have a sexual abuser right in your own home, or among family and friends. Your child will give you signs if he or she has been touched sexually. Not all children will come right out and tell you someone has sexually assaulted them. Why? Eight out of ten reported cases have been committed by someone your child knows and trusts.[3] So parents, be alert for behavioral changes in your child that might indicate sexual abuse. Look for physical signs of abuse; take your child to his or her primary care doctor and express your concerns. Ask your doctor to examine the child and run tests to see if your child has had sexual contact, and if so, any sexually transmitted diseases. Never second-guess: follow the signs. It could possibly mean sexual abuse. Get them help immediately.

Also, parents, keep your children close to you as much as possible. Sometimes our children want to spend the night at their friend's house. Only if you feel comfortable and know that the members of that friend's family really care about your child should you allow them to spend the night there. This is how a lot of sexual misconduct takes place. We allow our children to spend the night at the homes of others, knowing there are teenage boys or girls there who are interested in sex. Parents, don't you know we are accountable for our children? It is our responsibility to protect them. The message is clear: protect your child.

CHAPTER ELEVEN

Stop the Violence in Our Youth Today

Most of today's youth are headed for destruction, and headed there fast. We as parents want to blame the neighborhoods we reside in, the rappers, the gangs, and our society. Well it's time we as parents take control of our children and the environment around our homes, as well as the schools and the community. Do not turn a blind eye to your children when you know they are out in society doing harm to themselves and others. It's time we as parents confront wrong; our children are suffering, dying because of their wrongdoings. The pain of youth violence hits our hearts as parents when it attacks one of our own children. But in reality the pain of all violence—especially that involving our youth—should be in our minds even if it does not affect one of our loved ones.

It is important that we as parents realize teen violence needs to be stopped now because we are losing our children to the system, or to the cemeteries. Every day, we hear of teen violence on television, the newspapers, and the Internet. Recently, in September of 2009, a sixteen-year-old Chicago boy lost his life to teen violence. Derrion Albert was an innocent bystander when he was viciously attacked by a group of teenage boys. He was simply on his way home from school when four or five youngsters brutally beat him. They beat him with a wooden board until he was unconscious. He regained consciousness and tried to get up and move away from his attackers, but they began to attack him again. They struck him in the head with the wooden board again, kicked and punched him, and then they stomped on his head repeatedly until he lay lifeless. This young man lost his life because our young people have clearly lost their direction in life. He was an honor student in school trying to make something with his life.

According to the Center of Disease Control and Prevention, homicide is the second leading cause of death for young people between 10-24 years of age.[4] Parents, what is going on in our youth's mind that is leading them to kill, steal, and cause deep hurt to others, and to themselves? We as parents must ask ourselves this question. How many more of our children must lose their lives to this sickness? The way our children are behaving in today's society it is clear they don't understand what our ancestors went through under slavery. Our great grandparents and some of our grandparents fought to become free from slavery so that the young people today could have a brighter future. A lot of the youth today listen to the history of slavery, how our ancestors were jailed, and how many died fighting for freedom. But in reality the youth have not absorbed in their minds and hearts what really took place with slavery. It is our responsibility to give our children the knowledge about what really happened with our ancestors. Educate our young people about why they are even able to go to school to receive an education. Tell them why they can ride public transportation without being asked to move to the back of the bus.

I took my oldest son, Vonte, to Atlanta, Georgia, this spring break to visit the Dr. Martin Luther King Jr. National Historic Site. I know Vonte had read about Dr. King in school, but to actually see where he was from, and the house he was born in, took it to another level for him. Our tour guide was a preacher who'd actually walked with Dr. King during the civil rights marches. Reverend Williams was proud of this, and he took time to explain the purpose of Dr. King's legacy.

Dr. King wanted to make sure the youth today would be able to achieve their dreams and become whatever they wanted to become in life. He served jail time so that we might have equal rights. He dedicated his life to nonviolence. They told Dr. King that he would be killed, but he fought for justice and equal opportunity until the day he died.

Reverend Williams asked the youth present on our tour, "What is history?" It got very quiet in the room; the children didn't know what to say.

Then Vonte said, "Something that happened in the past, and something money cannot buy."

It is important for the youth to understand the struggle, and what it took to get to where we are today. The killings, and the brutal attacks our youth are going through today defeat the plan that every ancestor bled and died for. Parents, it is important that we take a strong hold of our youth in today's society. Let us as parents start a support system in our own homes. Start to supervise our own children more than we have in the past. Make sure that we become more consistent with our disciplinary practices. The only way the sickness can continue to plague our families is if we as parents do nothing about it.

On the anniversary of my grandmother's birthday in 2009, I took my children to visit her grave. As I looked around at the gravesites my heart wept; nearly half of them were filled with young people who'd died between the ages of seventeen and twenty-five. Not knowing the cause of death, I could only imagine how many had died due to violence. Today's youth are living in a world of make believe. Most of them don't care who they hurt—it's about this make-believe picture they have painted in their heads. We as parents know that's not the real world. Our parents worked for what they wanted, and we as parents work for what we want. Teach your children the difference between reality and fantasy. I believe our children are committing wrongful acts because they are living their lives in a fantasy world. It is our duty to give our children a reality check about what's happening in this world. Take one weekend out of your busy schedule to go with your entire family someplace where they can volunteer their services; perhaps a shelter or group home. Have your child do some type of community service in the neighborhood you live in.

Giving service to a group home, or a non-for-profit organization, will certainly give your child a different outlook on life in the real world. I guarantee your child will come back feeling some type of transformation. Everything given to your child will begin to be appreciated, just to see how blessed he or she is to have what a lot of people can't provide for themselves.

Are you scared to talk to your child about what's right and wrong? That's the question I want to ask. If you are afraid of your own child, I suggest you reach out to someone that your child respects as an authority figure and trust this person will not lead them down the path of destruction. If you are living in fear of your own child, then I know you believe society is as well. A lot of times as parents we do more harm than good to our children by just giving them everything they ask.

Not only does the child lose respect for you, he or she also loses respect for others and their belongings. Show them how to earn everything they receive from you. For every task that your child completes, let there be a reward. For example, for every "A" they earn in class, let them receive something they desire. Keep the rewards you give within reason, but try to demonstrate that no good deed goes unnoticed. Not only does that show children responsibility, it also allows them to understand the concept of being committed to every task or job they do. I too have been guilty of giving to my children without them earning it. You see, I know we feel we should do better than our parents did when we were growing up, which is not a bad idea because we might be capable of giving to our children. The problem with this, however, is that we as parents don't make them earn what they get. Keep it simple: with our children let's not complicate what society is really about. It's time to stop the madness among our youth, and this must start at home. If you realize the situation is out of control, then start seeking outside help for your child.

Whether you believe it or not your child wants to stop the violence. Maybe he's gotten in too deep, or maybe he feels that no one cares about what he says or does. Tell him you care; talk with him about the problems. You'll be surprised at the outcome when you communicate about his problems. If you don't attack the problem through communication children will build walls of defense against you. When a child begins to rebel, it is a sign that something is wrong in their life.

It could be as simple as a hug from you, or just a word of encouragement. How often, parents, do you take the time to tell your children that you love them? Even if they are not little ones anymore, it is important that they feel the warmth of that love. If your children are teenagers don't stop expressing your love to them. Even now, when I receive a hug or a kiss from my mom, it makes whatever difficult situation I'm dealing with go away. Just the tender touch of my mom infuses in me the idea of gathering strength to continue my day. I have a dad, but he is afraid I'm still upset with him. Dad, I love you, and I forgive you. Maybe you need to hear me say that. I will continue to bring your grandchildren to visit as much as I can. No need to carry shame or regrets; you are still my father and I am still your Mookie.

To the dads who are not at home, your voice can be powerful to your children. Dads, you are a strong element in their lives and you can be very helpful in keeping them away from violent behavior. I would like you to take a minute to think about the child you have brought into this world. If ever someone needed you, it is your child. They need to feel your presence in their life at all times. Fathers, don't think you don't matter—it's important to understand that you really do matter. Whatever happened in your life that now makes you feel unwanted or not received by your child, you are wrong: you are wanted and you will be received. It might take some time for the child to respond the way you think he or she should. You must become a listener; there might be a few things your children need to get off of their chests—allow them to do just that. A lot of times, fathers, you think if you didn't meet your child support obligations the child will reject you. I'm here to tell you that it is not true. Your child will welcome your love regardless of whether you come with or without money and gifts. It is important for you to build a personal relationship with your child, regardless of what you and your child's mother went through.

Yes, a lot of mothers feel the father should contribute to the child financially and by right they should feel that way, and you as the father should also feel the need to contribute to your child's needs and education. Yes, you might feel attacked by the mother when she requests that you pay child support. Don't feel attacked: just work on becoming able to contribute financially. Don't get upset and run away: try to understand that has nothing to do with the mental and physical support you give to your child.

Make a pact with your son that you will be there for him. Take time out each and every day just to place a phone call to your daughter. Don't ask to speak with Mom, because you already know that conversation might turn out to be an unpleasant one. Just stick to the most important part—your child.

Maybe you also feel guilty that you have not been there like you wanted to be in the past. Whatever kept you from being there in the past, let go of it: your child needs you to make an adult decision that you will be there from this day onwards. Deal with whatever guilt you have and start fresh. If an apology is long overdue, give the apology to your child. They have no control over grown up situations. Your son is out there in a gang, or on his way to jail, or robbing and killing people. Your daughter has ran away from home, and she's run into some man's arms because she's trying to fill the void of her absent father. Your children are staring death in the face. You need to reach out to them as much as possible to avoid the destruction awaiting them. You need to step between your child and the peer pressure he or she deals with at school. Keep your promise to your child. Take the time to learn who your child is, so that the two of you can build an emotional connection. You could have been absent from your child's life for ten years, but if you make up in your mind that you really want a solid relationship with your child, you could definitely have one. The only thing or person that is stopping that relationship between you and your child ***is you***.

Mothers, when dealing with child support and other similar issues, keep it between adults. Don't speak against the father to your children; it is wrong to do so, and it will drive a wedge between the children and their father. Encourage your son to speak with his father, encourage your daughter to visit her father. Sometimes, mothers, we have to take the first step to really show Dad that his child needs him. Even though you personally don't get along with each other, your child should remain your main concern.

So, fathers, here is what I would like you to do. Make yourself a weekly checklist:

1. Set your alarm clock and call your child before school to say, "Good morning. Have a good day in school." End the conversation with, "I love you." This takes just five minutes out of your morning.

2. Place another call to your child after school just to ask how the day went, did you receive homework, and end the conversation with, "I love you." This takes just five minutes out of your afternoon.

3. In the evening, place your last call of the day just to make sure your child is not out at late hours, that she's getting prepared for the next day, and end that conversation with, "I love you." This takes just five minutes out of your evening.

4. When the weekend comes around, plan ahead to do something with your child that doesn't cost you a dime. Perhaps you could take a drive just to have a one-on-one conversation, or you could go to the local park to play. If you

have a teenager, challenge him in a game of one-on-one basketball, or take her for a bike ride, or maybe your parents would like to see their grandchild. Have lunch at a relative's home. This will give your child a chance to know where he or she comes from. Return the child home if he or she isn't sleeping over; give a hug and a kiss. This takes just two hours out of your weekend.

5. Dads, you have cell phones as well; meet with your child's teachers, give them your cell phone number, retrieve each teacher's e-mail address, and make sure you know when the next parent-teacher conference is. If you don't wish to attend while the mother is around, go by yourself to see your child's teachers. Then speak with your child one on one about the conference you had with the teachers. You don't have to be a college educator or be very book smart. You just have to be a concerned father.

Now get back to whatever you were doing for the rest of your day. Business has been conducted. Whether you want to hang out with friends, go have a beer, get your high on, or sit on the street corner talking trash, that's your prerogative. Your children feel loved by their father and couldn't care less about the rest. Stop the violence with your child, or the chain will continue, but we need you fathers to help us keep the children of our future safe. They are your seed, your flesh and blood, and they deserve your support to keep them on the right track.

6. Dads, if you have a daughter, when it is appropriate for her to date, let her first date be with you. Show your daughter how she is supposed to be treated when a young man asks her out on a date.

Also, to prevent this disease that is spreading rapidly throughout our communities, involve everyone else you think might be of help to your child.

School officials, your city or town officials, volunteers in the Big Brother or Big Ssister program, members of the church, and most importantly, his or her primary doctor. Reach out to your children: they have lost their way and need your help getting back.

To community leaders, whom the people elected to serve to the community, I ask that you please get involved with implementing a plan for the youth in your area. Make sure the park districts have good youth programs. The youth programs you put in place should take into consideration activities the youth are interested in. Don't misappropriate for your personal gains the budget that has been given to you for the community. Adopt an attitude of bringing about change for the better of the community that elected you. That boy or girl might tell that gang leader: I pass—I'd rather go hang out at the youth center. You might not be able to reach every boy or girl; but for each one you do reach, you'll have fulfilled your duty. You'll be able to go home to rest knowing you have accomplished what you were elected to do. Remember, you have taken on a duty to be the parent for the community you believed was in need of change. That is why you took interest in political office: to bring about a positive change.

To school officials and teachers, I believe you entered this professional field because you have a passion for children, and for helping with their learning. Oftentimes I have heard teachers say, "I have too many students to let every parent know the progress of every child." I want to talk about a teacher's job description for a minute. Teachers are there to prepare materials and conduct classroom activities. Read to the students in large or small groups. Observe each student; examine performance, behavior, how each student relates socially, and physical well-being. Teachers, you become the parent in your classroom each and every day. You are to help your students individually, as well as in groups. When teachers observe any type of a behavioral problem, they are to inform parents, counselors, and administration in order to gain control over the problem. When a teacher sees that a student does not comprehend the lectures, the teacher should prepare and give tools to the student that will assist in learning. Teachers, please don't take the attitude that says, "I am here to just earn my paycheck." The student requires your support in order to learn. I understand your classroom might have twenty-five to thirty-five students, but you also should keep in mind the oath you took when you received your degree from college to do your best for every student that enters your classroom.

Don't be afraid to inform the parents of your students' progress, or for that matter their lack of progress. Don't wait until parent-teacher conferences to do it: get the parents involved at the earliest signs of trouble, whether it's a student's learning ability, or a behavioral or social problem. Take the time when you have parent-teacher conferences to collect e-mail addresses and cell phone numbers from every parent. This way you have more than a home number or address for the student. When parents come home from work they hardly ever check the voicemail on the home phone. Even if you send a letter home, parents may not get it: the child might arrive home before the parents and retrieve it. Teachers, just cover all grounds while the child is in your care. You want to have a solid relationship with every one of your students' parents.

To our spiritual advisors and the pastors of our churches: let's all go back to the old landmark of the church. It's okay to teach prosperity—we all want to gain wealth and receive a blessing that is true. But teach our parents a few times during your Sunday sermon about how to raise a child. In my opinion, not every sermon you preach has to be a yelling match. Take time to teach and educate your congregation about how to be good parents. Teach them how to deal with marital and parenting problems.

Often in church there are retreats for married couples, and sometimes for couples who aren't married. What about retreats that involve the children?

Have a retreat just for fathers and sons, and one for mothers and daughters, so that each parent can deal with issues they're having at home. Then switch the parents and have fathers bring their daughters, and mothers bring their sons, and discuss the same concerns. Talk about what the child is going through. If there are single parents in the church, ask the deacons, evangelists, and elders of the church to act as the other parent and accompany a boy or girl to the retreat. I believe that's one of the tasks that the deacons, evangelists, members of the mother board, and elders should assist the pastor with. Let go of titles in the church and let's get down to the business of saving our youth from danger.

Teach our parents positive messages that they can carry back to their homes. Help them understand that these messages should have positive effects on their children's lives. Mark 11:23-24 reads,

> ***For verily I say unto you, That whosoever shall say unto this mountain, Be thou removed, and be thou cast into the sea; and shall not doubt in his heart, but shall believe that those things which he saith shall come to pass; he shall have whatsoever he saith. Therefore I say unto you, What things soever ye desire, when ye pray, believe that ye receive them, and ye shall have them.***

Basically, parents, when you speak positively to your children, their minds develop positive energy. Teach them to have faith when they pray for change in life. First, the children must believe they have the power to do what they wish to do, become what they wish to be. Then, they must work hard at achieving these goals themselves.

I encourage every Pastor, Bishop—whatever your title is—to make youth a high priority. If you have a congregation of thousands, I suggest you have your secretaries pull out your Rolodex and start taking down names of every parent and child under your leadership. Don't just focus on who gives a big dollar to your church; focus on all the souls you preach to every Sunday. Perhaps you were blessed with a large congregation for a reason: God might have felt you would be capable of reaching out to each of those souls personally. Use the blessing God has given you. Don't take God's gift for granted; don't forget the purpose of your calling in the word of God.

CHAPTER TWELVE

Reality Check

Let's all get moving parents—we have work to do. This is about our future, our children. We cannot be defeated; we must conquer. It's time to strive for our children and their futures. Let us motivate one another as parents where our children attend schools. Let's get involved in what they are learning in school. What levels of math are being taught to our children, in their elementary school programs as well as high school programs? If we as parents start to get involved with our children's education, we can change things. Start with the schools, the school district offices, and the politicians—all the way to the White House. Where change has to be brought about let us move toward change: that's the only way we will win, the only way we can say a difference has been made.

Let's introduce nutritional diets in our homes and in our schools too. Let's be health-conscious for ourselves as well as our children. Sickness is taking over our lives. Leave the fast food alone. Parents, even after a hard day at work, you need to persevere and cook a healthy, balanced meal. Teach our children how to prepare easy healthy meals. Take time to read the ingredients of the things we and our children consume. It might seem like a hard transition, but once you get the hang of maintaining good eating habits, it will supersede artificial foods.

Give our children the message: no more killing. When parents lose a child, the community loses a child, and society too. No more robbing, or hurting others for what you think you should have. Speak up when hateful acts are committed—otherwise there will surely be a price to pay. Let us work together to show our children how to do good deeds for themselves as well as others. Before they can love anyone else, they must first learn to love themselves. Once they get the concept of loving themselves truthfully, they will love others as they love themselves. It will take them a long way in their life's journey. No good deed goes unnoticed—it will show itself and they will be rewarded. It has been written and the good book does not lie. The only way we can move forward with a positive attitude is by first accepting change. If we as parents continue to ignore the problems our children are facing, they will see nothing but destruction. Grab onto faith and believe that the work you put in on behalf of your own children and their future will pay off. Speak a positive message about life. Present them with good role models, starting with you. Then move on to the person you date or marry, the neighborhood you decide to move in, and the schools you select for them to attend. We as parents must make sacrifices for our children's future. If you move into a better neighborhood, it may mean that you might not be able to drive the best car. If you send your child to a better school, it may mean that you can't wear designer clothes. Basically, we might have to give up certain things that we cannot afford at the present time if it means a better way of life for our own seed. We as parents must put our priorities in perspective so that our children can be fruitful in this land we live in. We must nurture the seed we have planted on this earth. In order for a seed to grow it has to be nourished with positive energy. Parents, let us begin with a positive message about how to live life with our children. The late Dr. Evelyn Davis used to sing, "If you just hold out till tomorrow, if you just keep the faith through the night, if you just hold out till tomorrow, everything will be alright."

From my heart and mind to yours, I pray to you, let us be mindful of our children, let us love our children, let us teach our children, let us educate our children, and most importantly, let us be heroes for our children. God bless you, thank you for giving me the opportunity to deliver a message that I felt was long overdue. I pray for you as a parent and ask that you pray for me as a parent.

Remember My Child, My Reponsibility

* NIV Teen Study Bible

Footnotes

Page 11 [1] King James Bible.

Page 69 [2] Grades 1-6." Japanese Education System: Elementary Schools http://members.tripod.com/h_javora/jed6.htm. n.p., n.d. Web. 3 Feb. 2011.

Page 89 [3] "The Prosecution of Child Sexual Abuse in Idaho: July 1, 2006 – June 30, 2007." http://scholarworks.boisestate.edu/crimjust_facpubs/9/. Boise State University Scholar Works, 2008. Web. 22 Feb. 2011.

Page 92 [4] "Youth Violence." http://www.cdc.gov/violenceprevention/pdf/YV-DataSheet-a.pdf. cdc.gov, 2010. Web. 3 Feb. 2011.

MEET *the* AUTHOR

Jonetta Smith, author of the book "My Child My Responsibility," as her first book she focuses on what means the most, parenting and child development to adulthood. Jonetta is an advocate for effective parenting who holds several certificates in child development, and has worked in public administration. As a divorced mother of three teenagers, and as the diligent observer of a large and colorful family (full of mistakes, and triumphs), she is inspired to write for other parents.

Jonetta's practical, common sense approach to parenting and family management is keyed throughout her book. Her theology on supporting the physical, emotional, social, and intellectual growth of a child is unique and proves that parenting isn't just a biological relationship but rather a day to day activity.

Jonetta loves being able to teach and share her life experiences with other parents in order to help those souls going through similar times; "Consistency in prayer and effort will make a difference." She lives in Chicago, IL, with her children where she is owner of a real estate management firm and a writer. Jonetta has been guest speaker for the Student Career Day in Chicago's south suburban public schools, and Grace on Wheels teen parenting conference in 2011. She is quoted saying "Our children are crying out for help and we as parents should be the first to hear of their cries."

Take the Parent Pledge!

www.jonettasmith.com

~ A WORD ABOUT CHILD HEALTH ~

Throughout the book I strongly focus on what matters the most; family, parenting and child development, from infancy to adulthood. I encourage parents to slow down from day to day hustle and bustle operations of their life, to enjoy and embrace their child(ren) and receive the full reward of being a parent which is the most important role they will ever take on. I strongly believe that parent-child interaction and physical activity engagement is one of true virtues of being a parent; in that it gives parents the platform to exercise their parenting abilities to improve the health and well-being of their children's lives. Remember, good parenting requires good health and good parenting skills, why not start with the most important parts, our body and mind.

> *"Obesity on children is a major concern both in the United States and Worldwide including developing countries. It is the major cause of morbidity as well as hypertension, insulin resistant diabetes, osteoarthritis, and depression in individuals.*
>
> *The best way to prevent obesity in children is with personnel education concerning sedentary lifestyles, caloric intake (portion size), and increased physical activity. We need to have Pediatric and Governmental agencies work to make available structured physical activity by building environments that include sidewalks, parks, and playgrounds."*
>
> *– Cyrus Akrami, M.D.*

Meet *the* Family

The Smith family, (left to right), Jaylin, JaVonte', Jonetta, Graylin.

Motivational Speaker
Parenting/Life Coach Workshop

Author, Jonetta Smith, is available to conduct Parenting/Life Coaching classes in schools, churches, etc.

To schedule a seven-day parenting workshop in your school, or church, contact Jonetta Smith by email:

www.jonetta@jonettasmith.com

Follow Jonetta's parenting blog
www.jonettasmith.com/parentlounge

Jaylin and Jonetta's hair and makeup on all photos by Romona (Nicole) Peeples-Madison of Bun's Inc.

"You are forever with me..."

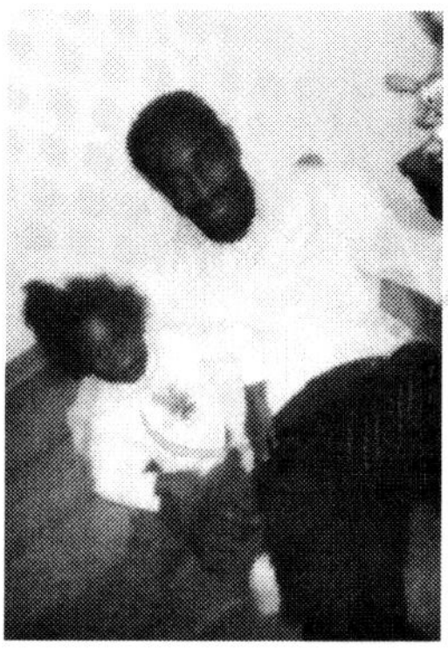

Daniel Reeves

October 11, 1922

November 5, 1980

Irene Reeves

November 30, 1924

October 24, 2006

Come hang out with Jaylin!

Jaylin's blog is just for teens.
Friends can drop by and air their thoughts and feelings.
Join the discussion or start a new conversation.
Come over and hang out today.

www.jonettasmith.com/jaylinsroom

Princess J Media

STAY IN TOUCH...

Keep up with Jonetta on all seminars, workshops, and upcoming engagements.

To order additional books, go to:

www.jonettasmith.com
or ask for it at your favorite bookseller.